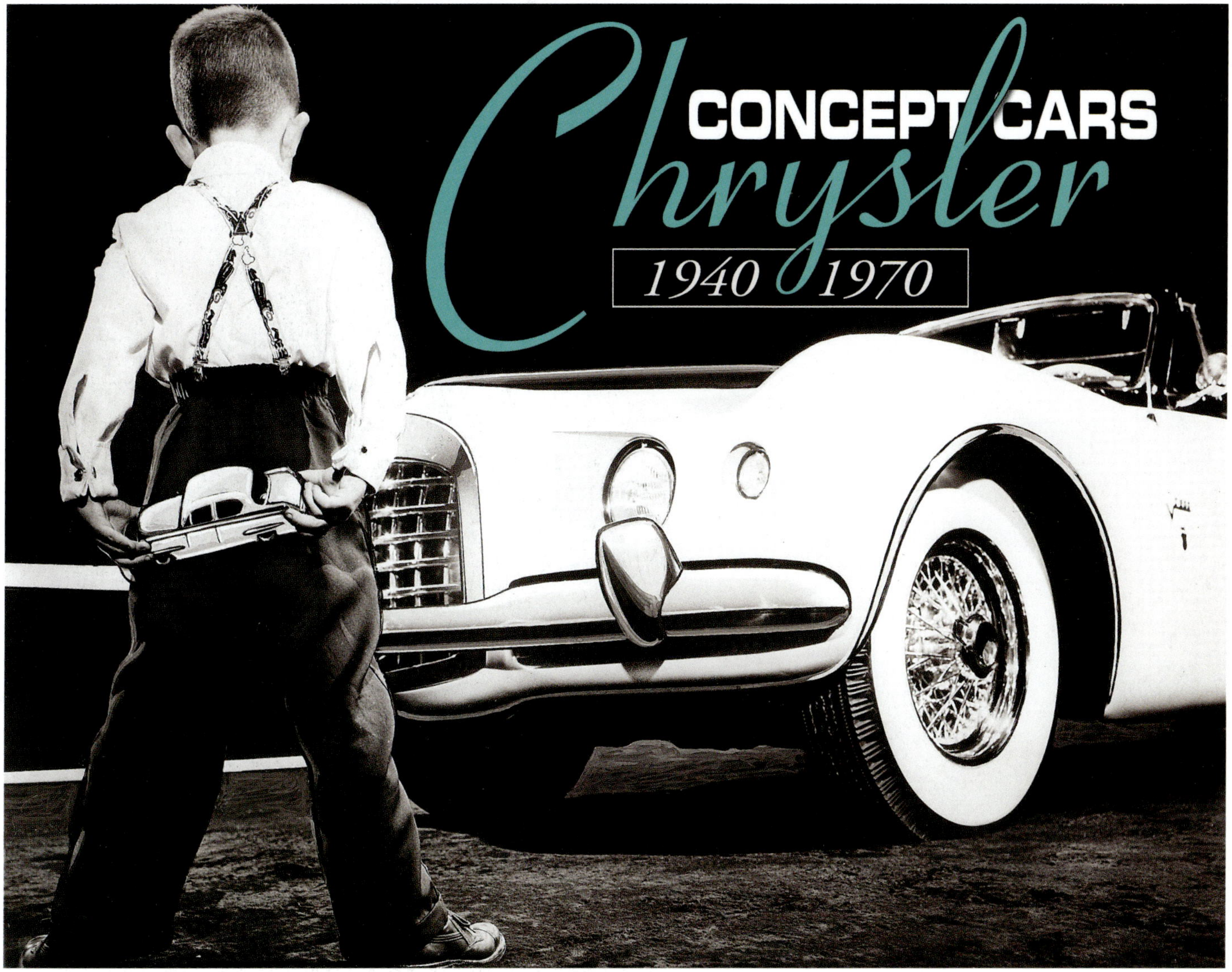

CONCEPT CARS

Chrysler

1940 — 1970

David Fetherston and Tony Thacker

CarTech ®

Edited by Peter Bodensteiner
Designed by Katie Sonmor

ISBN-13 978-1-932494-70-9

Printed in China

Cover: 1961 Chrysler Turboflite

Front flap: 1941 Chrysler Thunderbolt

Back flap: 1968 Dodge Charger III

CarTech®

39966 Grand Avenue
North Branch, MN 55056
Telephone: (651) 277-1200 or (800) 551-4754
Fax: (651) 277-1203
www.cartechbooks.com

Library of Congress Cataloging-in-Publication Data

Fetherston, David, 1950-
  Chrysler concept cars 1949-1970 / by David Fetherston & Tony Thacker.
      p. cm.
  Includes index.
  ISBN 978-1-932494-70-9
  1. Chrysler automobile--History--20th century. 2. Experimental automobiles--History--20th century. I. Thacker, Tony, 1949- II. Title.
  TL215.C55F48 2007
  629.222--dc22
                              2007043279

Acknowledgments

Compiling a volume of this magnitude requires considerable input from numerous sources, and this book could not have been written and illustrated without the valued contributions of a number of people. Not the least of these is Tom Gale, who gave purpose to the endeavor with his foresight and drive to reinvent the Chrysler Corporation, aided by his latter-day musketeers: Trevor Creed, John Herlitz, and Neil Walling.

Others who gave their time and resources include, of course, the DaimlerChrysler public relations staff; the staff of the product design office; and Brandt Rosenbush of the DaimlerChrysler archives, who endured our constant badgering to, "Just look for this one more image, please."

Also giving their time were Gerry Durnell of *Automobile Quarterly*, George Barris, Carrozzeria Bertone S.p.A., David Burgess-Wise, Dick Burke, Mike Chase, Bill Delaney, Don DeLaRossa, Detroit Public Library—National Automotive History Collection, Barry Dressel—Walter P. Chrysler Museum, Brandes Elitch, Bill Erdman, Sally Erickson, Antonia Kate Fetherston, Henry Ford Museum—Greenfield Village archive staff, David Freiburger, Barbara Fronzcak, Ghia S.p.A., Jeff Godshall, Ken Gross, the Jacuzzi family, Alden Jewell, Steven Juliano, Al LaCroix, Chuck Mashigan, Colin Neale, Mark Patrick, Petersen Automotive Museum, Pininfarina S.p.A., Art Ponder, Mike Nicks and Primedia, Bill Robinson, Brandt Rosenbush, Jon Rundles, Lee Seckler, Nanette Simmons, Jesse Simmons, *Special Interest Autos* magazine, Kailay Thacker, Thom Taylor, John Thompson Automotive Literature, Tom Tremont, C. Van Tune, the staff of *Motor Trend* magazine, and Al Turner and Bob Longstreth, who provided help, information, direction, and emotional support when it occasionally looked like this would be impossible to complete.

Special thanks are also extended to the fabulous coronary care team at Kaiser Hospitals in Santa Rosa, California and San Francisco, including Dr. Steve Werlin, Dr. Mario Pompili, and Dr. Scott Yang. You guys are the best!

Finally, we owe thanks to Dana Waterman, who took up the cause when sources appeared to be running dry. Dana worked as an engineer in the advanced studio between 1955 and 1965, one of the most exciting periods in Chrysler Corporation's glorious idea and concept car history. Dana was diligent in contacting his contemporaries and persuading them to share their stories, which make this book all the more interesting. Dana, we couldn't have done it as well without you.

If we have forgotten anybody, we sincerely apologize.

OVERSEAS DISTRIBUTION BY:

Brooklands Books Ltd.
P.O. Box 146, Cobham, Surrey, KT11 1LG, England
Telephone 01932 865051 • Fax 01932 868803
www.brooklands-books.com

Brooklands Books Aus.
3/37-39 Green Street, Banksmeadow, NSW 2109, Australia
Telephone 2 9695 7055 • Fax 2 9695 7355

Contents

Thank you to the following for providing photography and other materials used in the creation of this book:

Chrysler Historical Collection
Ghia S.p.A. Historical Archives
Pininfarina S.p.A. Historical Archives
Carrozzeria Bertone S.p.A. Historical Archives
Petersen Publishing Archives (Primedia)

Henry Ford Museum
Collection of David Burgess-Wise
Collection of Steven Juliano
Collection of David Fetherston

Foreword

To celebrate the life of one of the foremost automotive designers of the 1950s, we open with a 1954 presentation by Virgil Exner to the Chrysler sales staff. It was Exner who created a whole era of style at the Chrysler Corporation in the 1950s with designs that turned dreams into the dream machines for generations to come. Here are some of his thoughts. — *David Fetherston and Tony Thacker*

Nearly everyone is interested in automobiles. Someone once said that, at least among men, automobiles were the third most popular subject, exceeded in popularity only by women and politics… .

As a stylist, I'm happy about that. But this emphasis has a lot of misguided stimulation. It has come from our competition, who have a great deal to fear from the superior engineering of Chrysler Corporation cars. They have thus resorted to old and sound tactics, namely, divert attention from your weaknesses and make a lot of noise about what you think is strong about you.

Our competitors have had some success with this tactic, too. They have been able to persuade a lot of people that while Chrysler-built cars might be well engineered, they aren't well styled. Not well styled? By whose standards? By their standards, of course. Our competitors' alleged standards of styling are shared by no other designers of modern transportation. Our competitors themselves are evolving their styling standards and moving towards styling that follows the school Chrysler has long been supporting. Chrysler Corporation styling right now, today, is among some of the best examples of really modern, functional, clean styling to be found in the automobile industry.

First of all, let's look at some outstanding examples of today's styling in the tools we use for traveling. The modern railroad car is clean, functional, and straightforward. It is poised and has no ponderous look in spite of the fact that it is a massive piece of machinery. There are no phony shapes to make it look like something it isn't.

Look at the steamship United States. It is one of the largest, most massive pieces of machinery for travel ever built by man. Yet it, too, is clean, sleek, and almost lightly borne in appearance.

Virgil Exner, unfortunately with his eyes closed in this previously unpublished photograph presents the d'Elegance in New York.

There isn't an inch of non-functional, meaningless adornment to mar its beautifully styled exterior. And again, today's airliners reflect truly functional, utterly clean, and slender beauty. This is the meaning of modern styling for modern transportation.

I'm sure you see that amidst the automobile industry, there is a glaring exception to all this. It is the jellyroll and tinsel styling that has been touted as modern fashion in many automobiles. We might ask ourselves how well we have done our job of education when the only old-fashioned gingerbread design that still exists in modern products is found in certain popular automobiles.

Our competitors themselves are learning that time is running out. It looks like they realize that the public is fed up with so much gingerbread and bad taste. In last week's General Motors Motorama in New York City, GM stylists revealed some of their future-style thinking. Believe me, very few of their idea cars reflect traditional GM bathtub styling. The most significant GM cars of tomorrow were proof that Chrysler's dedication to styling with a lean and functional look has been correct all along. There can be no question that these GM cars of the future stem mostly from the Chrysler Corporation styling tradition.

Flatter body panels in the 1954 Olds, Buick, and Cadillac cars show that GM styling has already begun to move away from the traditional GM bulbous look. GM's 1954 look attempts to capture some of the fresh, clean lines that have been traditional with Chrysler. By letting them put us on the defensive in the past, we have allowed them to brand our functional styling as old-fashioned! I think we had better be on our guard, lest some day we wake up and find them producing styling in the Chrysler tradition and claiming they invented it! Let's make sure we don't let them convince the public that they originated the Chrysler functional look.

Compactness and slimness are something to be admired in a car, providing, of course, interior allotments are not reduced. An air of agility, or ready-performance of direction and purpose, are the goals we strive for in styling an automobile. We try to express this honest point of view in our styling. Our present cars have this quality, which can be simply termed functionalism. There is beauty of line and form.

We believe that this is what the motorist wants in a car. But he has been indoctrinated and misled by the constant pounding of advertising and merchandising carried on by our competitors. We might take a look at some of these phases, which are presently being "hallelujahed."

Panoramic vision is being hailed as the styling advancement of the century, both in beauty and increased vision. Low, flat hoods also increase driver visibility, thus are both functional and good looking. Even air scoops on our hoods are functional.

The absence of excessive chrome trim gives our cars a sincerity that sets them apart from the false and garish. You can trim a car much the same way you can a dog. You can end up with a clean agile figure or one that is considerably overdone. Our styling aims for the former.

Rear-end styling is a very important part of the entire automobile, particularly when you consider the time you spend driving behind other cars. Subconsciously, and oftentimes consciously, you are appraising the lines, taillights, and even the bumper treatment of the car ahead. Our rear decks certainly have distinction in form and a pleasing appearance, especially when compared to the high, abrupt decks on GM cars.

The large wheel openings on our cars are another feature which sets them apart from the slab-sided designs. It would be rather absurd to try to hide the wings on an airplane, so why hide the wheels on a car—after all one of the greatest beauty assets a car has is its wheels. Then there is the wire-wheel story, which we prefaced back in 1951, and it's surprising how fast the competition followed suit.

Large opening K-type rear doors, for ease of entrance and exit, are another feature which combines good looks and utility, and offers rear seat passengers greater visibility. Opening the doors of our cars, we find interior styling and fine fabrics that have delighted the car-buyer public. More and more new-car sales are being governed by women, and we styled the interiors of our 1954

cars with this in mind. Interior designs and colors have been carefully chosen to complement exterior paints. In many cases, exterior colors are carried into the interior to give a color-keyed or color-matched car.

The Plymouth Belvedere line uses a color-matched inside and outside. The other Plymouth lines are color-keyed to give perfect color harmony between exterior colors, interior colors, and upholstery materials. The Plymouth Plaza offers either a smart blue or green stripe to provide color variety and harmony. Other Dodge models, all De Sotos, and Chrysler series furnish beautiful, harmonizing color combinations. This careful, in fact scientific, color key results in a greater variety and freedom of choice for the buyer than ever before.

The increased availability of colorful fabrics and matched exterior paint is a most powerful selling point, but the competition is catching on fast, and if we neglect this sales advantage, they will soon be telling the public that they invented the introduction of varied colors.

In summing up, our cars are styled with a definite poised look. Their compactness and slimness represents a genuine character. We're not trying to set a fashion by introducing false bulges or gimmicks, and are definitely not trying to style an entire car around a trick windshield.

Pilots have an old saying about airplane design. "If it looks right, it flies right." The same holds true for automobile styling: If it looks right, it runs right. Our cars look right—they run right!

—*Virgil Exner*

Introduction **From the Ashes of Maxwell**

Nothing fancy about this designer's desk at Chrysler in the 1930s.

The beginning of the 1920s was a turbulent time for the United States. Within three years it had three presidents: Woodrow Wilson, Warren Harding, and Calvin Coolidge. The post-war world was still in turmoil; the new League of Nations did little to slow the unrest that still boiled in Europe and threatened to unravel America with its own social disorder. It wasn't until Coolidge became president in 1923 that the nation took a turn for the better. He announced, "The business of America is business." His vision was to help usher the country into the heady years of "Coolidge Prosperity" with a stock market that soared, industries that achieved miracles of production on the first great assembly lines, the highest incomes of any country, and a car for every man! The auto industry rode the wave, and there were dozens of manufacturers building cars all around the nation, but very few of them were financially healthy. Such was the fate of Willys–Overland, Maxwell, and Chalmers.

In the fall of 1920, Walter P. Chrysler founded the Chrysler Corporation in Elizabeth, New Jersey and housed it in part of Willys–Overland, a company he had been asked to rebuild out of bankruptcy. The challenge of rebuilding Willys–Overland diverted his attention away from this new venture, and the resulting first Chrysler automobile was not of the quality or innovation he expected. He shut the project down before it even reached pre-production. All was not lost, however, as it was at Willys–Overland that Chrysler met a trio of engineers who became the cornerstone of his new car and

company: Fred Zeder, Owen Skelton, and Carl Breer. They would be known as the "Three Musketeers."

Having gotten Willys–Overland out of bankruptcy, Chrysler moved onto a similar project at Maxwell and Chalmers. He placed the companies in receivership while he worked out a way to own the pair. All along, the Zeder, Skelton, Breer team was working on a new car that would eventually become Chrysler's first.

They teamed up with Rollin White of the Cletrac Tractor Company and White Truck Company to finish the project. The team worked in the Cletrac facility in Newark, New Jersey until late 1922, when the joint project came to an end. What they created was an innovative vehicle featuring a lightweight six-cylinder engine, hydraulic brakes, and a tubular front axle with advanced-engineered steering, which combined to create a state-of-the-art automobile.

Even after the support of White had been withdrawn, Chrysler continued to fund the design and engineering of the car at Zeder, Skelton, Breer Engineering, who owned the design. By this time, Chrysler possessed both Maxwell and Chalmers, and it was through Maxwell that he purchased both Zeder, Skelton, Breer Engineering and their new car—the car that would soon carry his name. The car still needed another year of engineering, and it was certainly this development time that created the quality that Chrysler desired. Even then, Chrysler was engineering-oriented rather than style-oriented.

In the depth of a January storm in 1924, the New York Auto Show opened without Chrysler's new car displayed. The car couldn't

be shown, because it wasn't in production. Not to be denied, Chrysler displayed his new brand intermingled among his Maxwell and Chalmers displays. Two cars were also displayed in the lobby of the Hotel Commodore, where Chrysler invited buyers, dealers, and bankers to view his new models. Outside, on a blocked-off section of a side street beside the hotel, he also offered one of the first "ride-and-drive programs."

In a twist of fate the new Chrysler turned out to be the star of the show, but even more important, Chrysler was able to show his new "concept" to New York bankers, who soon lent him another $5 million dollars to help him build 32,000 cars that first year.

Left: The five-cylinder radial engine installed in one of two Stars. It drove the front wheels.

Below: Despite the failure of the Airflow, Chrysler persevered. Innovative engineering and design packages are in evidence with the '37 Star below, which looked like a 2/3-scale Airflow. Two mules were built and tested extensively, mostly in northern Michigan.

Like its competitors, the company Walter P. Chrysler built was engineering-driven, and it was most clearly defined by the Airflow debacle of 1934. Technically innovative, the Airflow's advanced styling—Chrysler Corporation's first cab-forward design—now viewed as a design to herald modern design and construction methods— caused buyers to stay away in droves. It was too much, too soon.

Chrysler was not about to give up, though, and after the Airflow was finished, some of the engineering team were moved onto a new project under Chrysler director of research, Ken Lee. Known as the "Star Cars," these innovative prototypes featured a five-cylinder radial engine in what looked like a two-thirds-scale Chrysler Airflow body. During 1937, two front-wheel-drive "mule cars" were driven more than 200,000 miles, mostly in northern Michigan, testing this exciting design. Unfortunately, the project was abandoned at the beginning of 1942.

Meanwhile, something else happened to cause the company to try a different approach. Over on Mack Avenue at Chrysler's main body supplier, Briggs Manufacturing, Ralph Roberts had recently returned from England. He was encouraged by Alex Tremulis to make a pitch to Chrysler

president K.T. Keller to build a couple of special-bodied cars based on a Tremulis concept of "The Measured Mile Creates a New Motor Car." The pitch was made, and Keller was sold—but he wanted the cars completed in just 90 days.

The Newport and the Thunderbolt would be Chrysler Corporation's first modern dream cars.

1941 *Chrysler Newport and Thunderbolt*

The following interview with Alex Tremulis first appeared in Special Interest Autos *magazine, Number 28.*

"It must have been the early part of 1939 when we heard that the coming war in Europe would shut down operations at Briggs Manufacturing in England. Rumors were flying that the legendary Ralph Roberts, of LeBaron fame, would soon return to Briggs in Detroit. Ralph had been in charge of the design studios in England, and had been serving our major account—Ford of England—with great success.

John Tjaarda was in charge of the design studio in Detroit. This was in a red brick building on Mack Avenue. We were located on the fifth floor, with a penthouse on the roof. The penthouse—some 50 feet square—was our "showroom in the sky," where we presented finished models to such industry giants as Edsel B. Ford, K.T. Keller, and Ed Macauley. Styling at Briggs was almost a "goodwill" department, where we at Briggs could offer our clients a fresh viewpoint, free from engineering restrictions and dedicated solely to the task of inspiring top management for future models. Edsel Ford and K.T. Keller both used to refer to us as their Escape Machine.

For weeks, we underlings at Briggs gossiped over what we thought might happen when these two giants of the design profession, Roberts and Tjaarda—men of equal stature in the Briggs hierarchy—were forced to share the same office together. We assumed that the studio would be cut in half, with half of us in Tjaarda's group and the other half under Roberts. Naturally, both would want the best men. However, the problem never came up. Tjaarda's men were too busy on Chrysler, Ford, and Packard programs and simply could not be spared. Roberts never pushed the point. He gracefully merged with the existing structure, and began his own series of projects.

For a while, Ralph used the drawing board next to mine. He would always wear a meticulously clean smock while drawing. Some people have always credited Ralph with being the managerial genius of LeBaron, while downgrading his design ability. This was simply not true. Ralph had been associated with some of the greatest designers ever; Tom Hibbard, Ray Dietrich, Bob Koto, Phil Wright... and a host of others. Their collective design expertise had rubbed off on him; he knew every visual design trick in the game. And when it came to purity of line, he was an absolute perfectionist.

I used to watch him take a razor blade and retune the curve of a French curve or a plastic sweep in order to achieve the exact line he wanted. A deviation of a sixteenth of an inch on a full-size drawing of a roof

Chrysler Newport

sweep was a tremendous trifle that might require hours on end to rectify before he was satisfied. Bob Koto was the only designer I ever worked with who attacked the celluloid sweeps with the same vengeance as Roberts. I eventually found myself doing the same thing, always in secrecy, away from the ever-watchful eye of John Tjaarda. I didn't want him to accuse me of going over to the other side.

Ralph started out doing some strange design for fully enclosed scooters and things like mini-type, narrow-gauge three-wheelers. One Friday afternoon, he asked me for advice, and in a joking fashion I told him he'd been in England too long and that Americans liked long, low, swoopy monsters. I remember suggesting to him that since he was highly regarded by K.T. Keller, why didn't he work out two or three very advanced concepts—super custom LeBarons—and sell them to Chrysler as show cars. Briggs needed a gimmick to sell Chrysler and had come up with nothing.

I told Ralph that Chrysler had been smarting under the stigma of the catastrophic disaster of the Chrysler Airflow for too long. All of us referred to it as the "Airflop." It had set the industry back 20 years. I had seen John Tjaarda's years of dedicated effort, slowly brainwashing the leaders of industry into accepting streamlining, thrown out overnight. We were all ordered to retrench; to return to the old, staid silhouette we thought we were finally done with. If we could somehow erase this stigma of streamlining, then Chrysler's sins of the past might be absolved.

All we had to do was to design and build a couple of the hottest streamlined cars since Rome burned and slap them with a Chrysler nameplate. Ralph replied, "Whatever you say, don't call it an Airflop."

"Don't worry," I said, "I'll kill them with kindness, extol the virtues of the Airflow philosophy, and pay tribute to the engineering geniuses that designed it." I won't even mention the fact that Ray Dietrich, one of the greatest stylists of all time, wasn't even allowed into the Airflow room and that he was allowed only one designer, Herb Weissinger, to enter the inner sanctum. Poor Herb used to walk out daily in complete frustration and

Chrysler Thunderbolt

mutter, "Only God can make a tree."

I thought about my suggestion all weekend, and on Monday morning I showed up with what I have always considered my greatest masterpiece in the art of salesmanship. I entitled it "The Measured Mile Creates a New Motor Car." Ralph was quite excited and got on the phone to K.T. Keller. In an hour we met in the office of the vice-president of Chrysler Division, Dave Wallace. Mr. Keller joined us. I had prepared a series of rough pencil sketches that ran the gamut of land speed record cars from Major Seagrave's 203-mph Sunbeam and Frank Lockhart's ill-fated Stutz Blackhawk, to Seagrave's 231-mph Golden Arrow and Sir Donald Campbell's brace of evolutionary Bluebirds. I wound up with Captain George Eyston's sheer brute force Thunderbolt that had recently set the land speed record of 357 mph at the Bonneville Salt Flats.

Alongside each of the racecars was a quick sketch of an imaginary passenger car inspired by the land speed record automobile. Of course, all these passenger cars had one thing in common with those illustrious racecars of the past: streamlining. They were all very aerodynamic, and obeyed the basic laws of nature, established by Chrysler's own engineering staff when they developed the Chrysler Airflow cars. Ralph had decided that I was to make the presentation. It was utterly impossible for him to read my Egyptian hieroglyphics. I proposed that these passenger cars be unmarked with nameplates, as they were unmistakably

The Newport paced the 1941 Indy 500. With visible fender seams, the Newport went the Buick Y-job one better in that its fenders flowed all the way to the rear. Rarely shown with the top up, the Newport apparently had a very intricate top that required considerable effort to rise. It was stowed in a trunk behind the rear seats. The tiny rear trunk held mostly the spare tire.

This is a clear view of the Newport's dual-cowl arrangement.

Chryslers and represented Chrysler's philosophy that function dictate form. And that beauty is the by-product of sheer engineering integrity—as exemplified by Chrysler's forward-thinking policy in the taming of the wind. I went on for about half an hour like this, sounding more and more like an advertising executive than a designer.

Keller was excited about two names: Golden Arrow and Thunderbolt. Could we design and build two cars and introduce than at the auto show in less than five months? Ralph answered, "Yes, providing we get no interference and that the designs are left to Briggs/LeBaron's professional judgment." We explained that we would need at least 60 days for quarter scale clay model exploration and three or four months to build the prototypes at LeBaron. I interjected that Mr. Keller and Mr. Wallace should be the only two men involved and aware of the project, any more and we would still be scraping clay a year from now. They agreed.

Mr. Wallace then had his secretary call Captain Eyston in England... and turned the phone over to me. I exchanged greetings with the great man and told him we were going to build an aerodynamic masterpiece inspired by his Thunderbolt, and that we wanted to use the name. When asked about the style of the logo, I stated, "No logo, we will use two lightning streaks, one on each door." All he said was, "Capital. Bloody, bloody good." We could use the name. However, if the Thunderbolt ever reached production, then we would have to discuss a royalty arrangement. When I told Dave Wallace, he cried, "Promise him anything. We want that name." Imagine my excitement. Here I was, 25 years old, topping off a successful top-level meeting with my first trans-Atlantic telephone call.

People later asked me how on earth we got Chrysler—which had now retrenched in defeat to conventional silhouettes—to buy such an advanced program. Had Ralph Roberts and I walked in there with two beautiful proposals, our chances of success would have been a hundred to one against us. Because of the nature of the business, the cars would have been nitpicked to death and never seen the light of day. Instead, we walked in that day and we sold abstraction. We had only my crude drawings. We sold philosophy that day, not a pair of cars. Keller and Wallace squinted their eyes and tried to imagine what we were trying to design. They bought sight unseen what we hadn't even designed yet. Their primitive Airflow philosophy—which had reached deaf ears—was suddenly rekindled when we walked in. We had them at our mercy. It was good for all of us. Perhaps Chrysler had been right when it developed its Airflow. And it gave the illustrious house of LeBaron—a tragic child of the Depression—the opportunity to go out in a blaze of glory.

Back at Briggs, Ralph asked Tjaarda for his permission to use me on the project. Tjaarda half-agreed, so a quick call to W. O. Briggs and I was on loan to Ralph with the proviso that if Tjaarda had any crisis I would have to help him out. Ralph now needed a design modeler. Another quick call this time to Thomas L. Hibbard, one of the original LeBaron giants, and he had just the man—a young

Leather, chrome, and a full-width engine-turned dash with symmetrical round gauges made for a beautiful interior in the Thunderbolt. A left-hand glove box concealed controls for the headlights, top, rear deck, and more.

designer from Toronto—John Hampshire. A native Canadian, John had just finished a line of streamlined, customized trucks for Labatt's beer. He had worked in New York for Hibbard, so he was a natural. With this small crew, Roberts was ready.

The theme of the Golden Arrow presented a real problem. First of all, it had a 45-degree slant on its nose that terminated in a sharp point; it had huge blisters on the hood that embraced the overhead cam assemblies of its Rolls-Royce aircraft engine. And the wheel fairings were divorced from the body. Ralph soon decided that the theme was impossible. I suggested instead that we use for inspiration one of Gordon Buehrig's most beautiful design concepts ever, a double-cowled Duesenberg phaeton. Why didn't we build a double-cowled phaeton... only really streamlined? By a slight stretch of the imagination, it would have LeBaron blood in its veins.

I must have made an impact on him, because in three days of whirling away on the drawing board he had it. There it was, at least 97 percent of the final version. And he did it all himself. Hampshire in the modeling room began preparing the buck. This was complicated in itself, as it would have to be modeled in open cockpit form with the seats also modeled in quarter scale. There was neither time nor modeling help available to do it in full-scale. Everything now had to have four times the accuracy of a full-size clay. Actually, a full-size job is a lot easier to do; in quarter-scale, everything is reduced accordingly and only a super-critical eye such as Ralph's could compensate for scale effect.

In this area he had been well prepared. He had years and years of experience in building custom bodies using only a full-size body draft. Ralph had done something really difficult with the design of his phaeton. The front cowl was lower than the rear cowl; he purposely wanted a car with a split personality. He argued that the driver should feel he was driving a sports car, completely oblivious to the passengers in the rear seats. As for the rear passengers, they should be well protected from the wind with their higher cowl, and ride comfortably in chauffeur-driven splendor. The easiest thing for him to do would have been make both cowls identical and let it go at that. But the challenge was there.

When Hampshire and Ralph were doing the clay, they constantly made adjustments... only to find optical illusions as they walked around the model. The long front fender posed hinging problems. The engineers said it was a first. They suggested ending the front fender in the middle of the front door like everybody else. Ralph refused. He said, "We'll buy time when we go into full-size and figure something out. We just don't have to make it work." The final deadline was only about 10 days away. Ralph jumped on a plane and went skiing in Aspen, Colorado, for the weekend figuring that a couple of days away would give him a fresh edge on Monday. It was just what he needed. When he got back he cleaned up all the little trifles and made the schedule.

The Thunderbolt was more of a problem. Ralph started working on it concurrently with the Golden Arrow. But he wanted to try one radical idea that K.T. Keller just wouldn't buy. Ralph had flown in a rainstorm with a pilot whose plane had a strange windshield that swept out at the top instead of the bottom. This pilot claimed that rain water flew right off, and that this curious design eliminated wind noise, too. So Ralph decided to try this advanced aerodynamic feature on the Thunderbolt. But the Chrysler people just wouldn't go for it. K.T. gave him an ultimatum. They would forget the Thunderbolt completely and do only one car.

I had done some preliminary sketches of my own, which I showed to Roberts and Mr. Keller and he agreed to give me 10 days to see what I could do. This was at the same time that Ralph was having problems with the phaeton, so I worked independently. I made a few

Left: Ralph Roberts with his wife and mother in the Thunderbolt. Compare this car to the black one (below), and you can see that not all had the same Budd streamlined train-style-fluted rocker panels. Dual air intakes were hidden under the inverted bumper.

changes to his original concept. The first thing I threw out was the crazy windshield. But I kept the compact-retracting roof that Ralph had planned. Along the rocker panels, I added fluted moldings. A streamlined Budd train that was very popular then inspired that. And in 10 days I had the Thunderbolt, just barely, on schedule.

Keller and Wallace came in for the final showing. They were ecstatic, but could we build two show cars in only three months? We had to make the New York Auto Show. We knew we could. We were lucky; we had the finest layout body draftsmen in the world at Briggs. We had Mr. Voytypka as chief body engineer. He said, "Yes, providing there are no changes in the designs." It would be hell seven days a week at wide-open throttle. As for the Thunderbolt, Voytypka wasn't sure. No one had ever made a curved windshield that large before. I assured him that if our glass failed I would settle for a V-shaped windshield with flat glass. On that basis he agreed and the decision was made to hit the auto show.

Up to the very last minute the phaeton was called the Golden Arrow. Imagine my surprise upon my arrival in New York when I saw a different sign on it. It was now the Chrysler Newport. The initial first run of brochures was thrown out, and new ones were being printed in New York. We were so late. I had come to New York with two gold arrows that had been fabricated in our shops. I was supposed to place them somewhere on the car with a bit of tape. I put the arrows back in my suitcase. Chrysler's advertising men had decided that the car in no way resembled Seagrave's Golden Arrow. Someone hurriedly thought up the name "Newport"—a real stroke of genius.

At the show a very distinguished moderator in a tuxedo introduced both cars in a speech entitled, "The Measured Mile Creates Two New Motor Cars." He read my original proposal verbatim. I had a large sketch pad on an easel, and I would sketch the land speed record cars as the narration unfolded. A lovely model in a glistening gown would then stamp "Courtesy of the Chrysler Corporation" on the sketch and everybody, especially the kids, would start scrambling for mementoes. The press coverage was tremendous. A typical headline was, "Chrysler, the Pioneers of the Airflow, Are Now Pointing the Way to the Future." In our own little way we were erasing some of the stigma of the Chrysler Airflow. Eventually both designs went on tour and were seen by a reputed six million people.

GM, under Harley Earl, had up to that time been recognized as the undisputed leader in styling. At the same show, they were showing their famed Buick show car then known as the Y model. It was a very beautiful car with front fenders that terminated in the front door. Ralph had beaten GM to the punch by flowing the fenders of the Newport into a gentle continuous sweep all the way to the rear fender. The Thunderbolt, of course, was devoid of all semblance of fenders at all, except for a subtle bulge that indicated where fenders used to be. Both of our cars later exerted a tremendous influence on the direction that Detroit styling eventually took. Ironically, when I got back to Detroit after the triumphant auto show, John Tjaarda informed me that his budget had been drastically cut because of the coming war. I had been laid off."

Four Thunderbolts were built, with flip-up headlamps. Each was painted a different color. Six Newports were built.

1950 *Plymouth XX-500*

A change in leadership at Chrysler occurred as the calendar turned to 1950. K.T. Keller moved up to chairman of the board and Lester Lum "Tex" Colbert came onboard as president on November 3, 1950. It was Colbert and Zeder who moved to create a whole new image for Chrysler when they went looking for a new designer to lead the Art and Color Department. While they were figuring who and what they wanted, they became interested in investigating and using a body-builder in Italy to create an image car for them.

In an interview that appeared in the Oct.–Nov. 1972 issue of *Special Interest Autos*, Virgil Exner said, "C.B. Thomas, who was president of Chrysler's Export Division at that time, got talking to Pinin Farina over dinner one evening. Somehow they talked each other into letting Farina build this custom body on the 1950 Plymouth chassis. The car itself was nothing spectacular, and I don't believe it was ever brought into this country, but the cost was ridiculously low, even for that time."

According to Bruno Alfieri's history of Ghia, Fiat, in the middle of reorganization and with the money from the Marshall Plan, had formed an alliance with Chrysler. There was an intensive exchange of visits and some plans for integrated production, but nothing came of it. But when Chrysler was looking for somebody to build some research prototypes, Luigi Gajal de La Chenaye of Fiat gave C.B. Thomas two names: Pininfarina and Ghia.

Of course, at the time the commission was created, Henry King was the formal head of Chrysler styling and reported to the chief engineer. K.T. Keller had hired Exner as director of the Advanced Styling Studio in late summer of 1949. According to Richard M. Langworth, writing in the December 1985 issue of *Car Collector*, "He had maybe 17

Possibly never before published, these photographs from Pininfarina show the original concept sketch and a profile view of the car they built for Chrysler.

While the artwork denotes a 131.5-inch wheelbase, it is Chrysler designer and historian Jeff Godshall's opinion that there was no 131.5-inch wheelbase Plymouth chassis at that time. The artwork also says, "Expressly designed for Chrysler Corp."

The XX-500 was well crafted. Liberal use of chrome trim can be seen around the windows, along the sill, and around the radiused wheel wells and the rear trim. Note that the bumpers had Thunderbolt-style blades.

people in all, including the modelers, and about four or five designers taken from what used to be Chrysler's Art and Color Section."

"Chrysler contacted both companies," continued Alfieri, "and commissioned a trial prototype from each. Two Plymouth chassis were sent to Turin with two identical sets of designs; the commission had to be carried out to the letter, with only marginal variations where they were absolutely necessary.

"Mario Boano looked the designs over and immediately decided they could be improved. At the risk of losing the order, he wrote to Chrysler requesting authorization to carry out substantial modifications to the model. Thomas's answer was swift and clear, 'Do whatever you think best.'"

Pininfarina, in contrast, built its car according to instructions, or so we believe. The two photographs leading off this chapter, kindly supplied by Pininfarina and possibly never before published, show a rather homely, European-flavored sedan—though it was supposedly designed in Detroit—with a two-tier bumper possibly derived from the 1950 Plymouth Special DeLuxe. Apparently, the car was built atop a 1950 131.5-inch Plymouth chassis. The nomenclature on the hood said

"Chrysler 131," and the backside of the photograph indicates it was a "Berline" six-passenger sedan, meaning a formal sedan with a division between the front seat and the rear compartment.

A close look reveals the detail changes from concept sketch to reality. For example, the body side trim changed, as did the shape and density of the side window trim. Notice also that the bumpers, front and rear, appear to be fitted with rubber-tipped bullets. It's a shame the finished front of the car isn't visible, but these images are the only two available from Pininfarina. The cost was reported to be less than $10,000.

Across town, on Via Tommaso Grossi, Ghia had, of course, taken a different tack. Modified by Ghia's stylists, what became known as the Plymouth XX-500 was a boxy, upright four-door sedan with rather Cisitalia-like lines of the Italian production sedans of the time. It looked like a slightly stretched limousine, with its large rear quarter windows and high-crowned roof.

According to Alfieri, "The two prototypes were ready almost together and were sent to America together. Pininfarina had kept faithfully to the design, but Ghia had re-interpreted one of the models on an Alfa Romeo 6C 2500, which had been extraordinarily successful both with the judges and the public at the September 1949 Ville d'Este Concours.

Alfieri went on to opine that it was the quality of work and the low cost that struck the Americans, rather than the model's style. Among the XX-500's most prominent design cues were its squat nose (which featured finely detailed front fenders and headlights), large wheel wells, and bumpers with blades similar to the Thunderbolt. Chrysler records indicate the XX-500 was built on a 118.5-inch wheelbase chassis and not the 131.5-inch chassis of the Pininfarina job. As details of the latter are few and far between, it's difficult to be certain. Chrysler documents published on November 1, 1961, go on to say that the XX-500 was powered by a stock, 217-ci flat-headed 6-cylinder engine. With a single 1-barrel carburetor and a compression ratio of 7:1, it produced 97 hp at 3,600 rpm. It was backed with a 3-speed manual transmission. A fully functional vehicle, it boasted a leather and Bedford cord interior, and rode on chrome wire wheels fitted with 6.70 x 15-inch tires.

According to several reports from the time, Zeder was most impressed with this car even though it was a show car. The quality of the work and the detailing impressed him as much as its amazingly low $10,000 price tag. Besides, it was the best looking Plymouth in a generation. Exner also now knew that if he wanted "idea cars" built, then Ghia was the place to go.

Chrysler executives praised Ghia's workmanship and attention to detail. From left to right: R.C. Somerville, vice president and general sales manager of Plymouth; John Mansfield, president; and Robert Anderson, chief engineer. Nothing of the XX-500's design found its way to production, but its build quality and low cost would lead Exner to Turin for many of the company's future idea cars.

1951 *Chrysler K-310*

The K-310 is the basic root node of all modern Chrysler concept cars. It was the first "idea car" to emerge from the sixth-floor studio of the new, semi-secret Chrysler Design Studio, where Virgil Exner was following K.T. Keller's directive to "Remake Chrysler's image."

Exner quickly filled the new studio with some fine creative talent, including Cliff Voss, Maury Baldwin, and clay modeler Harry Petersen. Within a few weeks, their first full design project was underway. Codenamed K-310, with the "K" in honor of Keller and the "310" for the horsepower output of a "hot rodded" version of the about-to-be-introduced 331-ci Chrysler Hemi V-8.

The slick K-310 set the styling theme for the first five Chrysler Ghia specials, which were as intriguing as any European exotic—the boldness of Exner's design work merged with fine Italian craftsmanship to create a show-stopping concept car. Billed as a "Sports Sedan" with

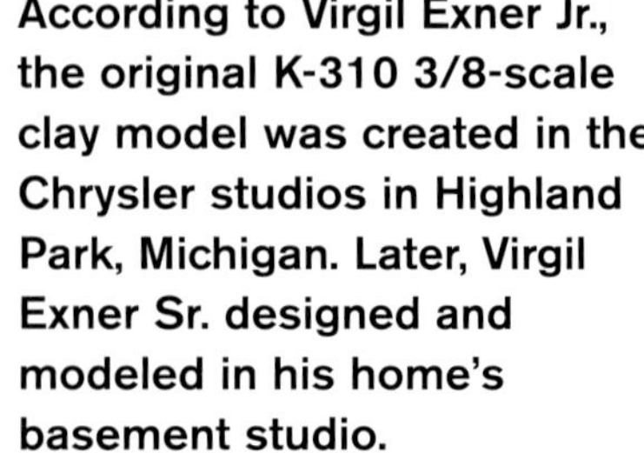

According to Virgil Exner Jr., the original K-310 3/8-scale clay model was created in the Chrysler studios in Highland Park, Michigan. Later, Virgil Exner Sr. designed and modeled in his home's basement studio.

From the clay, a plaster cast model was made and shipped to Ghia, in Italy, where the full-size was built in steel over a wooden buck.

This close-up of the clay shows the griffin and shield detail in the grille surround. The delicate egg-crate bars gave way to much heavier sections in the finished car.

seating for five, the K-310's long doors allowed easy access to front and rear seating. The front seat had an innovative 60/40 split that was designed to move forward as the back was folded down, allowing easy ingress and egress to the rear.

The K-310 turned out to be a large automobile at 220 inches long, but its sports coupe concept gave it a roof height of only 59 inches, which provided a delightfully compact look. The first sketches featured the spare tire mounted on the trunk lid, but this idea steadily evolved. Exner and his staff moved to produce a smoother look by sinking the spare wheel into the floor of the trunk, with a counterbalanced mount allowing the spare tire to be easily lifted out of the trunk floor. The end result was a stylized continental spare design element in the surface of

the trunk lid. Interestingly, this design element appeared in later Chrysler Corporation production vehicles, first on the 1957 Imperials and then on the first Plymouth Valiant.

The K-310 took approximately four months to work its way through the design process, from 30 rough sketches to final design renderings. During this process, a 3/8-scale clay was produced followed by a full-sized clay, which became the final design with only minor changes in the forms of the fenders.

At a time when most automotive designers were trying to hide the wheels, Exner chose to exaggerate them, saying at the Society of Automotive Engineers. Conference in Detroit in January 1952, "The wheel, one of man's oldest and most vital inventions, is also one of the purest and most beautiful designs. It is, likewise, the essence of functional automotive design. Why attempt to hide it?"

And hide them he did not, installing large diameter 17-inch triple-laced wire wheels fitted with 8.00 x 17-inch wide white-wall tires. Exaggerated with chrome trim around the wheel arches, the large wheels offered

Crowds flocked to see the K-310 in the showroom at the Jefferson Avenue assembly plant.

The finished car evidenced all of Virgil Exner's favorite themes, including the large, 17-inch chrome wire wheels mounted with wide whitewall tires, a stamped spare wheel cover in the decklid, and gunsight taillights, which more or less marked the rear extremity.

The 60/40-split front seats folded to allow ingress and egress of rear.

not only an interesting design cue but also allowed for larger brakes and a smoother ride, because of the compliance of the sidewalls. The wheels were set in floated pontoon fenders, with fluid bodylines merging the low hood line and bold front sheetmetal into a tightly conforming design with a body-contoured chromed grille.

In December 1950, Exner shipped Ghia a set of final sketches, specifications, and a series of 3/8-scale plaster models of the K-310 showing all exterior and interior design detailing.

To get the car built quickly, Exner decided to use a modified 125.5-inch production 1951 Chrysler Saratoga chassis. The chassis was shipped to Ghia in May 1951 complete with the then-experimental Hemi V-8 and the new PowerFlite fully automatic transmission, which would replace the production Fluid Drive semi-automatic.

With the car at Ghia, Chrysler Engineering continued to experiment with three other tuned "FirePower" Hemis. One was installed in a Kurtis-Kraft Indy Roadster owned by Roger Walcott. With Joe James at the wheel, the roadster set an Indianapolis Speedway record with an average speed of 135 mph for 140 miles.

Meanwhile, as the K-310 progressed at Ghia, knowledge of its existence spread, and Keller was apparently offered $400,000 for the car. Of course, Keller refused the offer outright, knowing full well that Chrysler's investment in the car was worth substantially more than just money.

The car was finished in early October 1951 and shipped to its first showing on November 2, 1951, in New York City at the Chrysler showroom in the Chrysler Building. A dockworkers strike in New York nearly scuttled its first showing, but some advanced organization resulted in the car being unloaded and transported to the showroom just in time for its official introduction.

The K-310 grille, including its griffin and shield ornamentation, the heavy chrome grille bars, and the bumper that encased it, was put into production on a number of Chrysler Imperial limousines—including one for Pope Pius XII.

1952 *Chrysler C-200*

Virgil Exner's next idea car, the C-200, was being rapidly completed at Ghia on the heels of the K-310's success. The C-200 was created as a six-seater sports car using the K-310 as its base. It used much of the K-310 body shape but with a convertible top replacing the hardtop, reshaped rear fenders and bumpers, and a new interior. It also included themes previously explored by Exner, including the gunsight taillights, huge wheel openings, and the impression of a spare wheel in the decklid. Interestingly, photographs taken at Ghia before the car was shipped to New York show it badged as a K-310. According to James C. Zeder, Chrysler Vice President and Director of Engineering and Research, "The C-200's style was achieved through flowing lines and careful integration of components. Chrysler designers have avoided throwing practical considerations to the winds merely to achieve fantastic styling for styling's sake."

According to press releases, "The C-200 was conceived as an experiment to explore the blending of sports car styling with practical automobile design that would measure up to an American driver's concept of how a car should handle and respond to local driving and traffic conditions."

As with the K-310, the C-200 was designed in Detroit. Painted and trimmed 3/8-scale models along with full-scale loftings were shipped to Ghia. Also shipped was a production 125.5-inch wheelbase Chrysler New Yorker chassis complete with the new FirePower Hemi V-8, suspension, and self-energizing disc brakes. Again, Exner chose 17-inch triple-laced wire wheels fitted with 8.00 x 17-inch wide white-wall tires.

Apparently, besides its excellent craftsmanship and reasonable costs, another reason Chrysler chose to use

The badge on the fender says "K-310," but the car became known as the C-200. Here, it has its top up and is surrounded by the Italian workers who built it. In the suits, left to right, are Mario Boano, C.B. Thomas, and Luigi Segre talking to the Italian press.

Ghia was its own heavy workload, caused by both defense and civilian research and production. This all was in the midst of the Korean Conflict, and Dodge especially was building large numbers of military trucks. So it was not a difficult decision to have Ghia create its new concept cars.

The C-200 was finished in less than eight months and shipped from Genoa, Italy, on the luxury liner S.S. *Constitution*, in time to appear on April 2, 1952, at the "Parade of Stars" Automobile Show at the Waldorf-Astoria

The interior was simple but the dash was busy with instruments and controls. Uncharacteristically, the speedometer was in miles per hour, and a left-hand tachometer read counter clockwise.

Hotel in New York City. The car went on to appear in Chrysler's touring show, "New Worlds in Motion," which visited some 15 cities each year.

Finished in light green and black with a black top, the C-200 was a classically styled open car with fine flowing lines, somewhat unfamiliar in Chrysler production cars of the time. The most interesting feature of the paintwork was how the colors were used to divide up the sections of the body. The hood and upper sections of the doors and rear quarter were trimmed in black, and this design enhanced both the folded tonneau and the top when it was erected. Overall, the C-200 measured 220.5 inches. It

This wonderful photograph courtesy of Ghia shows the C-200 with Luigi Segre on a small ferry, no doubt en route to Genoa from where the car was shipped to New York's West Side dock area aboard the SS *Constitution*.

padded safety pad. The seats were upholstered in two-tone leather and featured another example of the split-front-seat concept explored in the K-310. It was an idea that would rapidly find its way into production.

After the New York Auto Show was complete, the C-200 was shipped back to Detroit where it was upgraded with the new Chrysler power steering—the first power steering to both reduce effort and the number of turns lock-to-lock. The C-200 turned out to be an elegant design and met with great public acceptance.

stood 58 inches high and was a robust 79 inches wide.

The interior was designed to continue the sports car theme with a large tachometer and speedometer placed on either side of the steering column. Smaller dials for fuel, oil pressure, engine temperature, and amperes extended out to the right, along with a radio. Across the cowl and above the dash, was a leather-covered, foam-

In New York it was dropped on the dock side before being trucked to Detroit. Originally, the car was painted Jade green and black. And, according to *Car Collector* magazine, the Yugoslavs liked it so much it was featured on one of their postage stamps in 1953.

1952-53 *Chrysler SS*

The third idea car to result from the Chrysler–Ghia collaboration, the Chrysler SS (or Styling Special), would be the first to go into production, albeit in a modified form, and for the European rather than North American market.

According to an interview with Richard M. Langworth that appeared in the December 1985 issue of *Car Collector,* Virgil Exner Jr. said, "These two cars were designed in dad's basement in Birmingham [Michigan], and they were done as quarter-scale models, whereas the K-310 had been three-eighths."

Exner Jr. went on to say in his oral history, "I want to reiterate that while, in some cases, these show cars were actually drawn and designed by my father's own hand and actually modeled by him, especially the De Soto Adventurer, the Chrysler SS, and the D'Elegance to a great extent, for the most part any design effort, whether show cars or production, is a team effort."

Built on a New Yorker chassis cut down to a 119-inch wheelbase, the Special was powered by a stock 180-hp FirePower Hemi V-8 with a single 2-barrel carburetor and the aging Fluid-Torque transmission.

Riding on 7 x 16-inch chrome wire wheels with wide whitewall tires, the Special was the first design to feature Virgil Exner's innovative vertical bumperettes complete with side marker lights in the tips of the front and rear fender. Hydraulically mounted, they absorbed low-speed impact much like modern 5-mph bumpers.

The frontal treatment was far more detailed than the simple lines of the K-310 and featured, in addition to

Ghia artisans, including Luigi Segre on the right, Mario Felice Boano to his left, and Gian Paolo Boano next, give scale to the wooden buck. According to Richard M. Langworth in the December 1985 *Car Collector,* "Because the Italians had problems with the complex curvature of the fenders, those components were rendered in aluminum instead of steel. The 1953 version was of all-steel construction, Ghia now having apparently learned how to carve the beautifully shaped fenders."

The lines of the Special were even cleaner than those of the K-310 and the C-200. Gone was the "toilet seat," as some detractors called the spare wheel impression set into the decklid, along with the gunsight taillights. Instead, it was simple elegance, with the spare tucked behind the license plate. Note the forward-facing louvers in the cowl, push-button doors, and recessed Ghia badge.

the bumperettes, a horizontal bumper splitting, yet integral with, the heavily sculptured grille surround. Fine horizontal bars filled the grille, and a shield in the center carried a simple "X." The whole assembly formed a theme Exner would develop further for the 1953 De Soto Adventurer.

Chrome trim ran between the bumperettes and around the radiused wheel arches, and provided a natural color split between the two-tone dark green color scheme. There were no door handles—everything was push-button operated.

Forward-facing louvers adorned the tops of the fenders. In the case of the fastback, the fenders were, according to Langworth, aluminum rather than steel, "Because the Italians had problems with the complex curvature of

There were subtle differences between the 1952 and 1953 cars. For example, hood scoops replaced the fender-top louvers, there was a central power bulge, and there was a small, round badge containing the letters "TCS" and a Swiss flag. The letters could have stood for "C. Thomas Special," but according to Bruno Alfieri's history of Ghia, the car was eventually sold as the Chrysler ST-Special.

The instrumentation of the Thomas Special comprised two large, round composite gauges with the 220-kph speedometer on the right.

Trunk space, complete with upright spare, was more conventional of the Thomas Special than on other idea cars.

be packed on the rear seat. Bumperettes with small integral rear lights flanked the bumper, as did two chrome exhaust tips. Small flags adorned the rear fenders, and there were small, round bullet-shaped reverse lights set into the license frame just below the "Chrysler Special" script.

Designed as a two place/occasional four-place coupe, the interior was simple in design with a well-padded dark green leather bench seat split 60/40 to facilitate access to the rear seats, which could also hold a set of Italian hand-crafted luggage. The pleated theme was repeated on the door panels as well as the safety-padded dash panel, which had two large, round composite instruments mounted directly behind the steering wheel. According to Langworth, the speedometer was in kilometers per hour.

From end-to-end, the Special measured 214 inches, was 72.5 inches wide, and stood just 55 inches high. It made such an impact that C.B. Thomas, president of the Chrysler Export Division, ordered a second car built.

Rather than a fastback, the "Thomas Special," as it became known, featured a notchback design and is easily

the fenders." The front fenders also had a quirky character line that turned down from the fender top. It mirrored the leading edge of the rear fenders but was definitely an unusual treatment. The antenna sat in the corner of this depression.

If nothing else, the greenhouse predicted the shape of the historically significant profile that would appear on the following year's D'Elegance and also the Volkswagen Karmann Ghia.

The decklid, which contained a centrally mounted gas filler cap, sloped gently down to the chrome license frame before angling sharply down to meet the bumper. The license plate panel folded down to access the spare wheel, which slid out of its compartment along with a tool case. There was no luggage space, save what could identified by the use of conventional door handles in the place of the push buttons. Unlike the first Special, it was much more production-oriented and rode on an uncut, 125.5-inch wheelbase New Yorker chassis and 8.20 x 15-inch wheels. It was also much shorter, measuring only 204 inches overall. It was wider at 75.3 inches and taller at 57.5 inches. There were also minor differences in the bodywork.

While power was provided by the same stock 331-ci FirePower Hemi producing from a single 2-barrel carburetor, there was a new PowerFlite automatic transmission in place of the aging Fluid-Torque Drive. Also featured were production Imperial suspension, power brakes, and power steering.

Unlike the K-310 and the C-200, the whereabouts of which are unknown, both the original '52 Special and the '53 Thomas Special survive and have been restored. The latter currently resides in the Walter P. Chrysler Museum in Auburn Hills, Michigan.

The fastback version of the two Chrysler Specials was first displayed at the 1952 Paris Auto Salon, where it was well received.

Subsequently, Chrysler's Paris distributor commissioned Ghia to build a production version. Introduced in 1953 and called the GS-1, it used the same 125.5-inch wheelbase chassis as the notchback Thomas Special and was powered by the 331-ci, 180-hp Chrysler Hemi with a PowerFlite transmission and 8.20 x 15-inch tires.

Though it retained in essence the Special's styling, the GS-1 had a conventional front bumper in place of the one integral with the grille. The grille, though still with a wide chrome surround, was mounted higher and flanked with chrome-trimmed headlights. The side markers were moved from the bumperettes to below the headlights. Chrome side trim was also added, as was a character line above the fender. The rear was very similar to the Special, except that there was a conventional trunk with a standing spare wheel.

The GS-1 at its Paris debut. There were a number of changes made for production, including the addition of conventional bumpers and sill trim.

It is often said that 400 examples of the GS-1 were built for France-Motors, Chrysler's European dealer, but the survival rate is unknown. Bruno Alfieri's Ghia history also indicates that the vehicle evolved with production and that the last cars were built in 1954.

So as not to upset the domestic market, Ghia was forbidden to export the cars to the United States. However, the Chrysler chairman's son, Jacob Chrysler, ordered one car for his personal use, finished in Mountain Blue.

The GS-1 interior was likewise modified for production.

The inside of the Ghia facility in Via Tommaso Grossi, in the 1950s. In cramped quarters, a number of—perhaps as many as 400—Chrysler GS-1's were built alongside another successful Ghia model built upon the Alfa Romeo 1900 chassis. Interestingly, it used Virgil Exner's headlight design developed for the K-310.

The Storm Z-250

Though in no way a Chrysler idea car, the story of the Storm Z-250 is an interesting aside. In 1951, Fred M. Zeder Jr., an avid racer and son of Chrysler founder and "Three Musketeer" Fred M. Zeder (who, incidentally, died that year), planned to build his own dual-purpose car that could be equally at home on the road or track.

In partnership with Gene Casaroll of Automobile Shippers, Inc. and later Dual-Ghia fame, they formed Sports Car Development Corp. and planned to use as many Chrysler components as possible, including a Dodge Hemi engine.

Chrysler chassis engineer John Butterfield developed the chassis and suspension in the basement of his home while Chrysler designer Henry King worked on the body design and developed a quarter-scale clay model. According to Michael Lamm in his July/August 1994 story for *Special Interest Autos*, Virgil Exner would occasionally "drop over to Butterfield's basement to offer styling suggestions."

Over the Christmas vacation of 1952, Zeder Jr. went to Italy in search of a body builder, and chose Carrozzeria Bertone to do the work. A completed chassis was shipped to Italy in August 1953, but it was nine more months before the car was ready for testing. Nevertheless, it was displayed in the Turin Auto Show, where it won a first prize for style and design. The car was subsequently shipped to New York aboard the ill-fated *Andrea Doria*—she survived that journey.

In April 1954, Zeder Jr. took the car over to Chrysler, where his uncle Jim was chief engineer. Jim asked to borrow the car, now officially called the Storm Z-250. However, instead of the intended evaluation, Jim squirreled the car away with strict instructions that it not even be mentioned. The car was kept locked up for two years before it was returned to Zeder Jr., who then drove it regularly for 16 years. In the early-1990s, he restored the car, and it is now at the Petersen Automotive Museum in Los Angeles.

1953 *Chrysler D'Elegance*

For the 1953 season Ghia built two more idea cars derived from the original K-310 coupe. According to Virgil Exner Jr., his father developed these concepts, along with a quarter-scale model, working on his own at home in the basement. The D'Elegance carried a Chrysler badge while the Adventurer was tagged a De Soto—it was the first Ghia-built car to be called a De Soto. Although evidencing themes first explored in the K-310, both differed greatly in their details.

The D'Elegance was a smart-looking, three-seat fastback coupe—the third person had to sit sideways in the back—the lines of which were even more European with a smaller, distinctive greenhouse and more aggressive definition than either the K-310 or the C-200.

Standing just a tad over 54 inches tall and 214 inches long, the D'Elegance retained the peaked front bumper, which now eclipsed a larger grille with a "spinner" in the center behind the bumper. The single, round headlights

A disproportionate number of photographs of the D'Elegance 3/8-scale clay model survived, and they clearly show the development of the vehicle.

Front view, taken on April 24, 1952, clearly shows the form of the grille, the peaked fenders, and the recessed headlights, which also appeared on the '53 Ghia Alfa Romeo 1900C.

Here, in the rearview, taken on the same day, you can clearly see how the left side was taking shape compared to the right. You can also see the cut lines being made for the bumper recess and the license frame.

This rear 3/4, also taken on April 24, 1952, shows the character line that swept up into the rear fender. Note the scale wire wheels and the exhaust pipe. Note also the scale spare recessed into the decklid, which would appear later on production Imperials, Darts, and Valiants.

Left and bottom left: July 10, 1952, the clay was nearing completion, with all lines clearly defined including the bumpers, spare wheel covers, and license frame. Equally obvious is the yet-to-be-born Volkswagen Karmann Ghia.

with sharply defined eyebrows were likewise retained, but the body had much crisper lines and a heavy character line through the door and up into the rear fender. Incidentally, the recessed headlight treatment found its way onto the 1953 Alfa Romeo 1900C. According to Bruno Alfieri's

The spare-wheel mechanism occupied the whole trunk area, and comprised a hydraulic cylinder and accompanying linkage that lifted the spare wheel out from under the cover and lowered it down over the rear bumper. Note the exhaust outlets mounted under the bumper ends—compare this to the clay model.

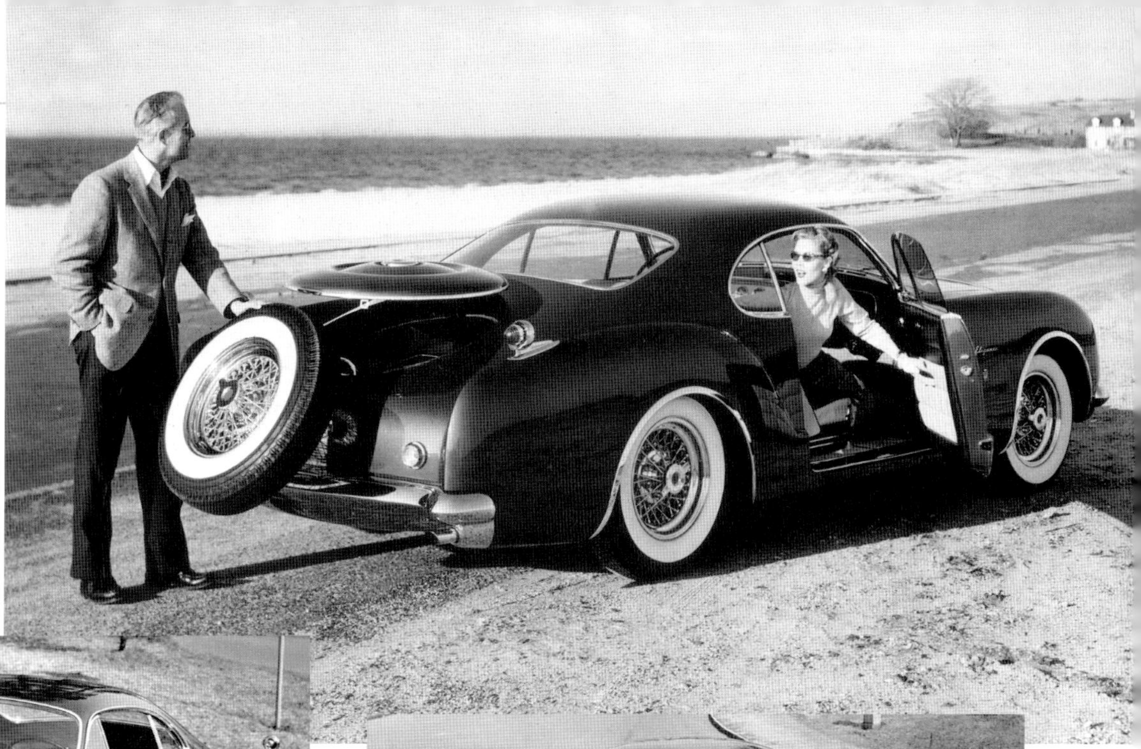

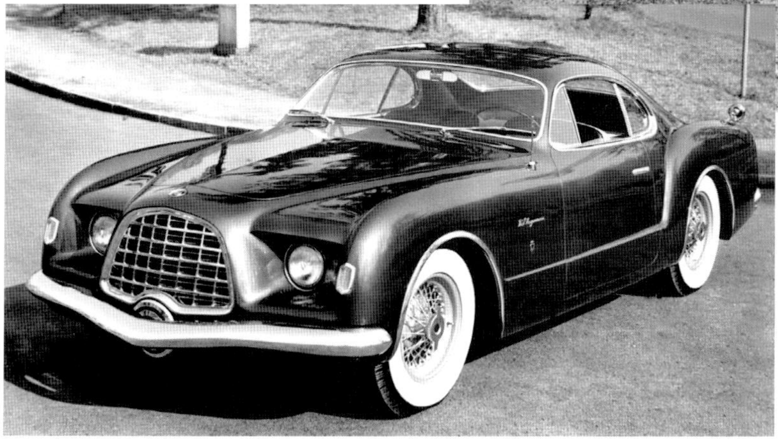

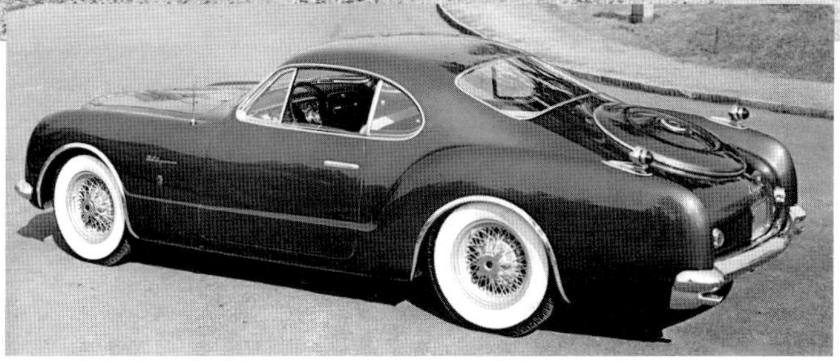

Gunsight taillights and back-up lights made up part of a busy rear end.

Ghia history, "The radiator grille and the air intakes which flanked it are in fact a Virgil Exner design."

However, it was the roof and the body-side character line that would provide Ghia a lasting legacy when it incorporated it nearly verbatim into the Volkswagen Karmann Ghia. According to Exner Jr., who visited Ghia in 1955, the top "was a direct, intentional swipe off the Chrysler D'Elegance. Giovanni Savonuzzi was the engineer and designer who downsized the D'Elegance and made the Karmann Ghia out of it. Nobody minded it. It was wonderful."

Exner's ideas first explored in the K-310 and incorporated in the D'Elegance included large, chrome-trimmed wheel openings filled with 7.60 x 17-inch

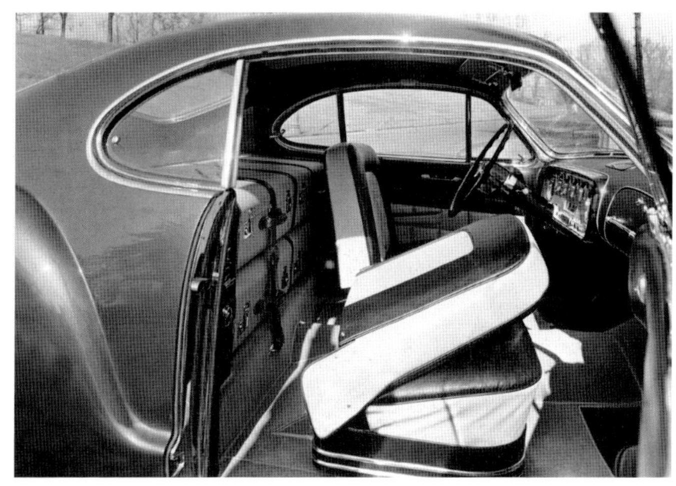

The 331-ci Chrysler FirePower produced 180 hp at 4,400 rpm with a single 2-barrel carburetor and Fluid-Torque transmission.

The elegant interior had room for two and their fitted English luggage. The instrument panel had the speedometer on the left in miles per hour and Chrysler's dash-mounted shift lever to the far left.

white-wall tires on chrome wire wheels, flush door handles, "gunsight" taillights, and a folding spare-tire mount. In this case, it lifted the spare wheel from its hiding place in the decklid under a disc covering, a feature that reappeared on several Exner-designed products later in the 1950s and early-1960s. Mechanical features included power windows and steering, and vacuum-boosted Ausco-Lambert self-energizing disc brakes that had been fitted to some Town & Country and Crown Imperial models late in the 1940s and early-1950s. Built on a modified New Yorker chassis that had been shortened 10 inches, to 115 inches, the powertrain featured a stock 180-hp FirePower 331-ci Hemi V-8 and a Chrysler four-speed Fluid-Torque automatic transmission. Later, the transmission was replaced with a 2-speed Chrysler PowerFlite.

The interior featured a wide, two-tone black-and-cream bench seat with a 60/40 split for easy access to the custom-made, yellow-and-black "fitted" English leather luggage. The symmetrical instrument panel was mounted to the left and contained six round-faced, white-on-red gauges—speedometer in MPH to the left; fuel, amp, oil, and temp gauges in the center; and a large clock to the right. There was a push-button radio set in the panel, and Chrysler's own in-dash gearshift lever protruded from the leather-covered fascia on the left-hand side of the instrument panel. Interestingly, the interior of the D'Elegance and most of the interiors of the other Ghia-built idea cars were left to Ghia to finalize using just a few preliminary sketches from Exner. When the project came to final trimming, Exner or Cliff Voss oversaw the final specifications.

Instead of debuting in a major American city or auto show, Chrysler introduced the D'Elegance at the 39th Annual International Automobile Salon in October 1952, in Paris. The car was so well received that Ghia put it into limited production, selling a reported 25 of them in Europe. Several of those are known to have survived.

Upon reflection, some D'Elegance design cues did find their way to production models. For example, the grille opening and ribbing certainly became the source of grille texture on some of the Chrysler 300 models, and the gunsight taillights appeared on the 1955 Imperials.

In January 2001, a bright-red restored D'Elegance (it was originally painted "Spring Coral"—a light metallic red) was sold at the Barrett-Jackson auction in Scottsdale, Arizona, for $310,000.

1953 *De Soto Adventurer*

Though similarly proportioned to the D'Elegance, the De Soto Adventurer, unveiled to the public on November 12, 1953, was quite a different and more restrained car, at least if one ignored the side pipes. Although it was built on a 4-inch shorter, 111-inch wheelbase, and measured 189.8 inches overall, it enjoyed balanced proportions and was a full four-seater. It was also a favorite of Virgil Exner, who said in an interview with John Lamm shortly before his death, "It would have been the first four-passenger sports car made in this

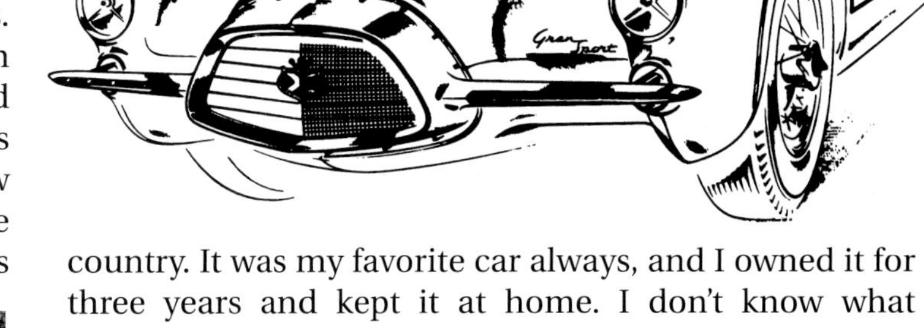

country. It was my favorite car always, and I owned it for three years and kept it at home. I don't know what became of it—I think it eventually went to a wealthy collector in South America."

Powered by a 170-hp, 276.1-ci De Soto FireDome V-8 with a single 2-barrel carburetor, the Adventurer stood 53.5 inches tall and was 67 inches wide. In the words of its contemporary press release, the car had, "an air of unlimited capability." The engine was coupled to a Fluid-Torque transmission. The car also enjoyed power steering and brakes.

The rear view of the Adventurer was quite unlike those of the other K-310 family, having a large wraparound backlight, no spare tire form in the deck—instead there was a large racing-style gas filler—and no gunsight taillights. The car was actually very simple and conventional, with few adornments other than the side pipes.

As had the three preceding K-310-inspired cars, it featured a front bumper that peaked over the grille, which, in turn, resembled that of the '52 Chrysler Special. It was separate from the front sheetmetal, which, in turn, flared out above the bumper to form flanking air intakes. However, unlike the K-310 family, the Adventurer had conventionally styled and mounted round headlights with chrome rings. Below the headlights were conventional round parking lamps.

Also unlike the preceding cars, there was no chrome trim around the radiused wheel openings. Instead, the wheel openings were slightly flared over the now-usual white-wall tires mounted on chrome wire wheels. Unlike the D'Elegance, the wheels on the Adventurer were 16 inches in diameter and were fitted with 6.70 x 16-inch tires. The front fenders did, however, display the "notch" at the cowl, common to all four cars, as well as having the defined haunches in the rear. The door handles were conventional and were not flush like those of the D'Elegance, and gone were the "gunsight" taillights, along with the form of the spare in the decklid. In its place a large "quick fill" filler cap was mounted on the centerline. The spare was accessed through a panel in the decklid. There was no trunk. For a car with so few exterior adornments, the exposed side-exhausts were somewhat

The Adventurer's bold chrome grille, inspiration for the 1960 De Soto grille, protruded from the front panel, which flared out to incorporate flanking air ducts.

anathema, but Exner would try them again on the 1955 Falcons.

Inside was a 2+2 with bucket seats front and rear, described in the January 1954 issue of *Motor Trend* as a "novel seating arrangement." The seats were covered in black leather with light-colored piping. The front seat backs folded forward to allow ingress to the rear, where the seats were upright buckets with three well-defined armrests. It had a conventionally laid out, full-width dash that employed seven standard De Soto instruments. They were round and were laid out symmetrically behind the steering wheel.

Though Exner, according to Exner Jr., "Always thought [the Adventurer] was one of his nicest designs," it didn't reflect American taste of the times and so, like most of Exner's idea cars, remained just that and never made it to production. Nevertheless, Exner drove the car for three years, and according to Don Kopka, who worked with Exner in the 1950s, he once took it to a concours at Lime Rock race circuit. It was so different from all the other cars in contention that a special class had to be created for it.

1953-54 *Dodge Firearrow I-IV*

Two small photographs on page 10 of the July 1953 issue of *Motor Trend* show a front three-quarter view and the interior of the Dodge Firearrow at its debut at the Turin Auto Show earlier that year. The Firearrow was a new direction in many ways from the precedents set by previous idea cars. The design was an obvious departure, and that is no doubt due to the fact that it was styled at Ghia, not Chrysler.

To begin with, the original car was a styling mock-up only and did not run, as did previous concepts. Gone were the pronounced "hips" of the Virgil Exner-penned K-310 series. In their place were dramatic, torpedo-like pontoon fenders sectioned with a chrome bumper, described by Michael Stevens in the November 1954 issue of *Motor Life* as a "chrome bellyband." Though new to America, Ghia

Gracing the cover of *Motorsport*, the first Firearrow looked to have a metallic purple paint job.

The "chrome bellyband," as it was often described, looked as if it was painted rather than chromed.

Chrome or paint, the trim ran all the way around the car. Those exhaust outlets were fake—the first Firearrow had no engine.

experimented with this treatment on other vehicles, including the Lancia Aurelia of the same year.

The Firearrow was also the first idea car since the Newport and Thunderbolt to not ride on chrome wires. It also had a frameless windshield and twin tailpipes exiting through the rear fender directly behind the rear wheel. These were not a new idea and were reminiscent of those on the Hudson Italia. Incidentally, Hudson used Touring as its Italian design house.

When the car was introduced to the American public at Chrysler's New York showroom later that year, an estimated 38,000 people came to view it and ask when they might buy and take delivery of one like it. The response was such that, in the January 1954 issue of *Motor Trend*, Don MacDonald stated, "The Firearrow can now be purchased on special order, according to a recent announcement by L.L. Colbert, Chrysler president. Delivery time is estimated at six months, and we understand the line will include a hardtop. No price was given."

In the November 1954 issue of *Motor Life,* Stevens stated, "According to current planning, Dodge is going to ship 100 chassis and engines to the Ghia factory in Turin, Italy, where they will be outfitted with Ghia bodies and other Italian touches, inside and out."

Unfortunately, Stevens was as out of touch with reality as Colbert was over-optimistic. In the May issue of *Motor Trend*, MacDonald, in his "Spotlight on Detroit" column, revealed that, according to Dodge President Bill Newberg, "This is the end of the line." There were no production plans.

The desire for a production Firearrow was obviously there, though, and Chrysler funded four versions (two roadsters with different front-end treatments, a coupe, and a convertible), which eventually led to the production of the Dual Ghia of 1956.

In or out of production, with or without an engine, the Firearrow roadster was an impressive concept. Painted what could have been candy red—it certainly had a metallic base—contrasting with a soft-yellow leather interior trimmed with maroon piping, the first car was dramatic with its all-enveloping bumper emerging from the aerojet-style intake grille like a propeller. Bob D'Olivo, writing in the November 1954 issue of *Motor Trend*, said, "A broad, sharp-edged band of chrome is almost the only applied decoration on the Firearrow. It is perhaps the most successful meeting of European and U.S. designs."

Dual Ghia

Eugene "Gene" Casaroll, the wealthy owner of Automobile Shippers, Inc.—a new-car shipping company—and a regular entrant of Indianapolis, had a plan to purchase Dodge chassis from the factory and ship them to Ghia, in Turin, Italy. There, Ghia would install convertible four-passenger bodies similar in design to the Firearrow.

The Firebomb (an unfortunate choice of names) was, according to Don MacDonald in the May 1955 issue of *Motor Trend*, "A direct descendant of the Firearrow." The prototype, powered by a 220-hp Dodge V-8, was unveiled at the 1955 Geneva Auto Show. It was introduced to the Detroit press at the Grosse Point Yacht Club on June 28.

The Firebomb had a 115-inch wheelbase, weighed a mere 2,700 pounds, and was completely belly-panned. The body was welded to the frame, and Giovanni Savonuzzi engineered the entire project. Production models were expected to have a wrap-around windshield, although the show car did not. Orders were taken at Dual-Motors' Detroit showroom, and some 117 examples were said to have been sold.

Built on a production 115-inch Dodge passenger-car chassis, the Firearrow was one of the first cars to incorporate dual headlight installations. This oval-mounted pair sat low to the ground under the bumper molding. MacDonald commented in his column for the January 1954 issue, "They are illegally close to the ground for use in most states." True or false, it hardly mattered on what was ostensibly a "pushmobile."

As noted, public reaction caused plenty of action, and Firearrow II, another roadster, quickly followed, though basically the same "chrome sandwich" detail changes abounded. The dramatic "aero" grille and "wraparound" bumper gave way to more conventional treatment. The propeller theme was replaced with a sim-ple crossbar—with small Dodge Coronet-like trim—that extended out to the fenders, where single round head-lights hung precariously. The side trim remained, as did the frameless windshield and the tailpipes, which were now functional. The rear end was similarly freshened with the removal of the chrome trim and the addition of new round taillights. The wire wheels were fitted with 7.10 x 15-inch tires, as were all the Firearrows.

Under the sleek exterior, this time painted pale yel-low, was a 119-inch Dodge Red Ram chassis, which had been substantially modified to accommodate the ultra-low 36-inch-high body. Power was provided by a stock 1953 241-ci Red Ram engine producing 150 hp (per Chrysler press releases) at 4,400 rpm.

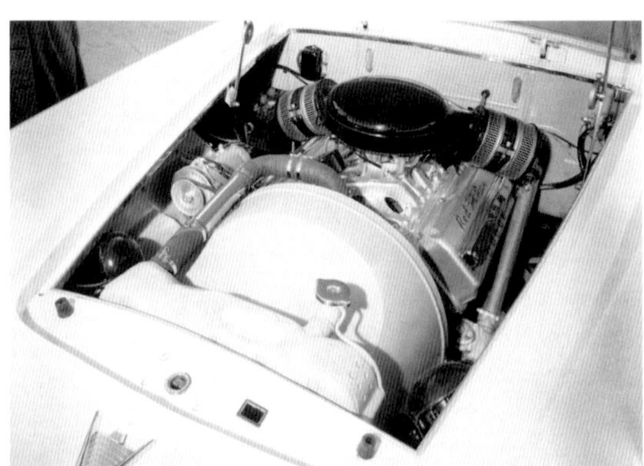

The Firearrow II differed greatly from its predecessor. Gone was the propeller-like center bar, replaced by more conventional trim. Gone also were the low-slung twin headlamps, replaced by single round units "frenched," according to Michael Stevens in *Motor Life*, into the very ends of the fenders. However, the essence of the "chrome sandwich" remained, as did the frameless windshield. Unlike Firearrow I, Firearrow II was a driver. Stevens tested it for *Motor Life* and said, "I kept in mind that the new PowerFlite transmission would have increased performance significantly."

In their November 1954 issues both *Motor Life* and *Motor Trend* purported to have test driven the Firearrow, but certain quotes raise the question of validity. *Motor Trend* ran a photograph of Firearrow I, and Bob D'Olivo talked about driving a car built in 1953 that was obtained from a Dodge showroom in Pasadena, California. Apparently, the car had a 1953 engine and a GyroTorque transmission. He said, "The car has more punch than stock, being lighter (3,200 pounds versus 3,680 for our test Dodge), giving it a better power/weight ratio."

D'Olivo went on to say that, "Three can sit abreast," which—because it had a wide, single black leather seat, as designed to seat three across or two with the huge center armrest pulled down—would indicate that he was writing about the second car. "A wooden-rimmed, racing-type steering wheel," was installed, along with a simple fascia housing two large round instruments, simple controls, and a centrally mounted radio. Interestingly, the stock column shift was retained.

Michael Stevens, in his test for *Motor Life*, likewise did not get the opportunity to put the Firearrow to the test, saying, "The car had barely 100 miles on the odometer and Dodge officials were, not unnaturally, reluctant to have it driven flat out." To sum up his "impressions" Stevens stated, "The Dodge Firearrow, on the street, attracted more attention, more startled looks, more pointed fingers than a runaway Japanese fire truck." But what was even more fascinating about this second Firearrow roadster was its width—it featured a 6.5-foot cockpit.

Hot on the heels of the second roadster came an equally dramatic coupe extolling all the finesse of an Italian exotic. The greenhouse—a variation of the D'Elegance top—was tight but abruptly formed up front, where there were fresh-air vents above the windshield. The backlight wrapped clear around and under the side windows.

In the rear, the styling was the same as the previous two cars except for the addition of twin "bumperettes," like those of the Ghia-built Lancia Aurelia. These

1954 Dodge Firearrow III

The Firearrow coupe displayed some interesting interior features. Large, round composite instruments were nestled low on either side of the steering column, which retained the column shift lever. Machined knobs resembling impeller blades controlled auxiliary functions and there was a swoopy art deco-style rearview mirror mounted on top of the dash, just above the radio.

diamond-pleat upholstery trimmed in black and white, which added drama to the car's brilliant red bodywork. Other innovative interior ideas included a removable rear seat that created a cargo area behind the front seat, much like an early Chrysler Town & Country trunk. The previous two roadsters had the spare located in a rear

bumperettes were repeated in the front, where there was a new grille sans crossbar. It was flanked by twin round headlights recessed in the style of the K-310. Firearrow III was indeed a precursor for both the De Soto Adventurer II and the Plymouth Explorer that followed closely behind.

Riding on another 119-inch chassis, the coupe was eventually powered by a 245-hp "hopped up" Hemi. In 1954, with aviatrix and race car driver Betty Skelton at the wheel, the coupe set a Closed-Course USAC Record of 144.4 mph at the dedication of Chrysler's new Chelsea (Michigan) Proving Ground. *Motor Trend*, in its August 1954 issue said, "Who says show cars don't run and women can't have a lead foot?"

The fourth and last in the series was the Firearrow convertible, which was basically the Firearrow coupe with the roof removed. However, it was a four-seater rather than a two-seat roadster. It featured unusual trunk, while another trunk between it and the cockpit housed the luggage.

The exterior of the convertible was very similar to the coupe. Journalists described the grille as "floating." Another strip of trim was added to the sill and the windshield, which now sported a heavy chrome surround.

Rearview mirrors were mounted on top of the fenders.

Again mounted on the 119-inch chassis and fitted with the 150-hp Red Ram V-8, the convertible was as close to a production car as could be. Chrysler demonstrated that a good, solid design concept could be evolved into a production model.

1954
Chrysler Le Comte and La Comtesse

"Anything less … Yesterday's Car!" screamed Chrysler's 1954 print ads. And, in many ways, the Chrysler La Comtesse and its male equivalent, the Le Comte, were indeed yesterday's car. The De Soto Adventurer II, Dodge Firearrow, Plymouth Belmont, and Explorer were all one-off Ghia-built cars, but the Le Comte and the La Comtesse were modified production New Yorker DeLuxe Newport hardtops. The styling was essentially six years old, and sales of all Chryslers at the time were falling dramatically. No doubt, these custom versions and the addition of some much-needed horsepower helped the '54 New Yorker DeLuxe outsell its 1953 counterpart by nearly 25 percent.

Production-based though they were, the cars were intriguing in their day because of their roof treatment, which comprised a large, contoured Plexiglas panel set into

The modifications made to the pink and gray La Comtesse comprised primarily the roof treatment, shown to greater effect on the opposite page on the Le Comte, and the continental spare from the Dodge Royal.

the steel top. In and of itself, this treatment was not unusual. Mercury and Ford had it in a production car and Cadillac in its Cyclone show car. However, it was new for Chrysler.

The exterior also featured a custom heavy-chrome molding running along the lower body of the car from the front wheel openings to the rear bumpers. The rest of the bodywork was stock New Yorker, including the brightwork and grille. At the rear, both cars were equipped with a new continental spare-tire mount from the Dodge Royal line.

Both cars were given the two-tone treatment. The La Comtesse was finished in Dusty Rose Pink on the body and Pigeon Gray on the top. A matching luxury interior was trimmed in cream and Dusty Rose leather with the seat back featuring platinum Brocatelle fabric. More masculine, the Le Comte was painted bronze and black.

Power was supplied by a 235-hp FirePower V-8, and the use of this more powerful engine signaled the start of the horsepower race. Chrysler raised the ante with new cylinder heads, 4-barrel carburetors, and dual exhausts. The transmission was the new, fully automatic PowerFlite. Finally, Chrysler's "high-roll" front suspension, along with new power steering and brakes, smoothed out their drivability.

1954 *Plymouth Belmont*

Not since the Newport and Thunderbolt parade cars of 1940 had an American company had the honor of building one of Chrysler's growing fleet of idea cars. However, as Chrysler neared the purchase of its major body-stamping supplier Briggs, in 1953, that situation changed, and Briggs embarked upon a project that would be made of fiberglass rather than steel.

Although employed in the '53 Corvette and by small-volume manufacturers such as Glaspar and Muntz, fiberglass was quite a departure for Briggs, a steel-body supplier since the turn of the century. It was used to test the practicality of fiberglass body fabrication while creating a zestful show car, much in the manner of the first Viper roadster concept built 40 years later.

The Belmont, shown here in Azure Blue at Chrysler's Chelsea Proving Grounds, alongside a pair of Firearrows. With a model alongside, the scale of the Belmont is obvious. Length was 191.5 inches, width 73.3, and height 49.3. Underneath was a 114-inch-wheelbase Dodge chassis, a 240-ci motor, and Plymouth's Hy-Drive transmission.

The Belmont had half doors, a storage compartment behind the cockpit for luggage, and a detachable fabric top.

The project was handled by Al Prance, chief designer at Briggs. Not only a departure in materials, the Belmont displayed many of the European influences of preceding idea cars. Indeed, it was very American too, with its lavish use of chrome trim and Corvette-style cockpit. The latter featured aviation-style bucket seats finished in white leather. Between them was a console housing a radio and an electronically controlled antenna—a first for Plymouth.

Other unusual features include the half doors and a detachable fabric top, which had to be removed before it could be stowed away in the trunk compartment along with the spare. The luggage compartment was subsequently placed ahead of the trunk in a separate compartment where the top would normally be stowed—not a very practical

Now restored and photographed at the Blackhawk Museum in 2002, the Belmont is resplendent in red with a gray interior. Originally, the interior, including the bucket seats and center console that carried the radio controls, was upholstered in white leather, and the exterior was Azure Blue.

Wherever it was shown, the Plymouth Belmont drew an admiring crowd. Overall, the Belmont measured 191.5 inches. It measured 32.75 inches to the tops of the doors and was 73 inches wide.

solution. The Belmont also employed a stand-alone, wraparound windshield with no side windows, much like a contemporary Italian sports racing car.

Built on a production 114-inch Dodge chassis fitted with a 150-hp, 241-ci Dodge Red Ram V-8 and a Plymouth Hy-Drive transmission, the Belmont first appeared finished in Azure Blue. However, over the years it has been repainted several times, and at the time of writing was a deep cherry red. Incidentally, the Belmont sported the ubiquitous 15-inch chromed wire wheels picked up from the Imperial line. The Belmont also featured "hipped" rear fenders that rose up into tail fins capped with small vertical taillights. Chrome trim ran the length of the car.

Introduced at the St. Louis Auto Show in 1954, the company's press release stated, "You can look to Plymouth for great things in today's cars—and tomorrow's." Tomorrow's indeed, for it would be many years before any Chrysler products would use any plastic body components. In retrospect, the Belmont was a landmark car for Plymouth. Not only was it on the cutting edge of construction at the time, its graciously full lines created a masculine design that has stood the test of time rather well.

1954 *Dodge Granada*

The mid-1950s was one of the most innovative periods in the history of the modern automobile. Not only had engines evolved from flathead to overhead valve, but fuel injection had arrived, manual transmissions now had competition from fluid-driven automatics, and steel was not the only body material.

Fiberglass was the flavor of the month, with several Detroit manufacturers dabbling in this new composite plastic technology. For example, Briggs built the Belmont for Chrysler out of multiple fiberglass pieces, much like a conventional stamped steel-bodied car.

Unlike previous fiberglass-bodied cars, the Granada, a joint styling and construction venture carried out by Ionia Manufacturing and Creative Industries, was molded in one piece less doors, hood, and decklid. The bumpers, structural members, and body-attaching brackets were also made of fiberglass.

Chrysler's other fiberglass concept car, the Granada—also debuted in 1954—took what had been learned from the Belmont exercise and evolved it into a new body-tooling innovation, a one-piece body unit. Ionia Manufacturing and Creative Industries in Michigan molded the body—less the doors, hood, and trunk—as a single unit. In this case, the grille, rockers, bumpers, structural members, body attachment brackets, and aprons were likewise fiberglass.

According to Don Mitchell, president of Ionia Manufacturing, "The Granada was the first purpose-built plastic car designed to fit directly onto a production car chassis. The Granada was most notable because other fiberglass cars have required as many as 80 component parts to assemble, but the Granada was built with just seven."

The styling was attributed to Briggs Manufacturing and was not generally applauded. Painted turquoise green, it was pertly aggressive and featured peaked head- and taillights, an operating convertible top, and regular window lifts. Built on a 114-inch Dodge chassis and powered by the 150-hp, 241-ci Dodge Red Ram Hemi V-8, the Granada was 76 inches wide, 55.5 inches tall, and measured 211 inches overall.

The Granada was unveiled on January 14, 1954, at the Los Angeles Auto Show by Dodge President William C. Newberg, who said, "The Granada is an experiment in plastic sports car styling as part of Dodge's continuing program to keep abreast and ahead of new developments in the auto industry." He also left no doubt with the audience that "steel would continue to be the main body-making material for years to come."

The Granada was recently in the Mitchell (Ionia) auto collection in Owosso, Michigan, and has been fully restored. Mitchell is the remaining offspring company of Ionia Manufacturing, the Granada's original fabricator.

1954 *De Soto Adventurer II*

Penned by Ghia engineer/designer Giovanni Savonuzzi, the De Soto Adventurer II was a complete departure, with the exception of its proportions, from its predecessor, designed by Virgil Exner.

Finely crafted and original, Adventurer II was unparalleled at the time, combining the best features of a great European GT coupe with hearty American power. During its introduction, Mr. L.I. Woolson, De Soto president, noted, "We believe that our styling people are leading the industry in creating a brand-new theme. They have taken some of the most desirable features of the continental sports car and translated them into a thoroughly American automobile."

In 1954 Turin, Italy saw the debut of the De Soto Adventurer II. In the middle is Virgil Exner, on his right is Giovanni Savonuzzi, and on his left is Luigi Segre. Ghia managing director Signore Casalis is behind and between Exner and Savonuzzi.

Standing just 55.5 inches high on a 125.5-inch wheelbase '54 De Soto FireDome Sportsman hardtop chassis fitted with 15-inch chrome wire wheels, Adventurer II had a small greenhouse, not dissimilar to the D'Elegance. All similarity ended there, though. The stretched, bumperless body had the look of a land-speed stream-liner with its long, low lines, round bodywork, semi-enclosed wheels, and jet "after-burner" taillights that would eventually see production on the '61 Thunderbird and

It has been said that the car had a bumper, but the car never appears to have been shown with one.

Chrysler's turbine cars (the T-Bird and turbine cars had the same designer, hence the similarity).

The front-end treatment was unique, with a wide, chromed egg-crate grille, single heavily shaded headlights, and no bumper. Apparently, there was a front bumper, but the car was never shown with one fitted. Other interesting features included the ribbed vents in the front fenders, De Soto nose trim, and crossed Italian and American flags on the rear quarter panels. More interesting was the huge rear window that could be retracted into the trunk. The extreme fastback roof had little of the "notch" common to traditional coupe rooflines.

The powertrain consisted of a 276-ci FireDome Hemi V-8 and a PowerFlite 2-speed automatic transmission. The chassis used production De Soto hardware with power-boosted brakes, and Gremmer worm and roller steering. However, it did use lowered springs with stock unequal length A-arms in the front end and a leaf-sprung solid rear axle.

Interior features included heating and air conditioning, black-and-white cowhide leather bucket seats, wool carpeting, a large center console fitted with most of the interior controls, a radio, hydraulic power window lifts, and one of those delightful 1950s exotic car touches—custom-fitted luggage. The dash was also quite unconventional for the time, with the top and front surface covered in grained, non-reflective black leather with pods trimmed in machine-turned chrome that surrounded the stock De Soto instruments.

The Adventurer II was quite a hit on the auto show and dealer circuits through 1956. Later that year, it was the centerpiece at the Brussels Auto Show in Belgium, and it was there that it was sold to the Chrysler distributor in Casablanca. Apparently, King Mohammed V of Morocco fancied the coupe, but after a two-week test, he declined to buy it—he couldn't fit his bodyguards and himself into the car.

The car then sat in the dealer's showroom for the next three years before being purchased by Art Spanjian. Art shipped the Adventurer II home to Ohio, where his local Chrysler dealer put it on display as a showroom attrac-

tion. The car was apparently sold to Dale Grove, of Ohio, and then to Armand Archer Sr., who drove it to Florida, where it stayed in dry storage for the next 25 years. In 1986, it was restored and has been part of the fabulous Behring Auto Collection in Danville, California.

Giovanni Savonuzzi

Giovanni Savonuzzi began his illustrious career at Fiat Avio, working in aeronautics alongside the great Fiat designers Gabrielli and Cisitalia D46 designer Dante Giacosa. In fact, it was Giacosa who recommended Savonuzzi to Piero Dusio to fine-tune the D46. In 1948, when the Cisitalia project was completed, Savonuzzi went freelance and became an assistant lecturer on automotive engineering at the Turin Politecnico.

He came to Ghia when Mario Boano and his son Gian Paolo had a disagreement with Luigi Segre. The Boano's planned to buy out Segre, but the plan backfired and Segre purchased their shares. Finding himself without a designer, Segre hired his friend Savonuzzi as technical director.

Savonuzzi's arrival gave Segre the expertise needed to push Ghia to the forefront of its profession. Savonuzzi hired Sergio Coggiola, Sergio Sartorelli, and Bruno Sacco, who for many years headed Mercedes-Benz design. Savonuzzi went on to create the Supersonic. Built first on a Fiat and subsequently Aston Martin and Jaguar chassis, the Supersonic was so successful that Segre sold it to Chrysler, and it became the genesis of the De Soto Adventurer II introduced in 1954 at the Turin, Italy show. It confirmed Ghia as an independent design house.

1954 *Plymouth Explorer*

Featured in the "Lost & Found" section of the February 2000 issue of *Classic & Sports Car* was what Mick Walsh described as an "ultra-rare Fiat 8V Ghia Supersonic." To the casual observer, the Fiat looks remarkably like the Plymouth Explorer of 1954, and Walsh went on to say,

"The original Supersonic (although not christened that then) was designed by Giovanni Savonuzzi for a Swiss client to clothe a Conrero Alfa chassis entered in the 1953 Mille Miglia. The Marquette was made of plasticine and turned over to Ghia to build the body. The Alfa's styling was then adapted for a small series based on the Fiat 8V chassis to be built by Ghia.

The Plymouth Explorer rode on chrome plated 15-inch wire wheels with simulated knock-off caps. The parking lights and indicators were mounted in the V-shaped rub strip that ran the length of the car. Under the long hood was a 230-ci Plymouth PowerFlow six. With a single 2-barrel carburetor it produced 110 hp at 3,600 rpm. Note the split front bumpers, a grille that rolled under the front, finely detailed headlights, and air vents in the header above the windshield.

Unlike other early Chrysler idea cars, the Explorer had a conventional decklid and usable trunk space. The rear end also featured an unusual combined taillight and tailpipe assembly.

The Explorer's seats were trimmed in eggshell white leather piped in black to contrast with the light green metallic exterior. Interestingly, the radio controls slid out of sight. At the push of a button, a panel dropped down to cover the opening.

Custom-built fitted luggage was another feature, although the car had more trunk space than most early Virgil Exner idea cars.

The design was launched at the 1953 Turin show, but the number built is not clear. Some claim five, others just two. As well as Fiats, the Supersonic style was fitted to a Jaguar and an Aston Martin chassis. One body was even retro-fitted to a 427 Cobra chassis by John Willment. An American, Paul Farago, bought the first car at Turin."

When Plymouth debuted its version at the 1954 Washington Auto Show, 200,000 people saw it and most of them loved it. The Explorer's styling picked up on numerous design themes popular at the time, including the jet age, with its huge, forward slanting jet-like intake grille; recessed headlights; and heavily molded side trim complete with air outlet. The latter was divided by chrome trim, which extended all the way to the tips of the rear fenders. The rear-end treatment was unusual in that it combined taillight and tail pipe assemblies. The lights were set into the rear fender extensions with round bezels that surrounded the dual exhaust pipe outlets.

Standing 54.5-inches tall, the Explorer measured 185.2 inches long and 76.9 inches wide. It was built on a 114-inch Plymouth chassis and, unlike almost all other Chrysler/Ghia concepts that were V-8-powered, was fitted with a stock, 230-ci Plymouth PowerFlow 6-cylinder producing a mere 110 hp. The transmission was a Hy-Drive automatic.

The interior was quite unique, with black piped "eggshell" white leather upholstery, aluminum-spoked wood-rimmed steering wheel, and an innovative dash. The dash featured a radio with controls that slid away out of sight when not in use—a feature that reappeared from at least one European manufacturer in the late 1990s. The four instruments included a clock with stop timer.

While little if anything of the Explorer's styling transferred into the Chrysler products of the 1950s, the large, open-mouthed grille idea did appear on the 1960 New Yorker and Saratoga.

1955 *Chrysler Falcon*

It is amazing that Chrysler was able to restrain itself when Chevrolet introduced the Corvette and Ford punched out the Thunderbird in two short model years, especially in light of the fact that Chrysler had, to its credit, an amazing array of conceptual two-seater sports cars. Argue though he might, and despite the fact that three versions of the Falcon were built, Virgil Exner's dreams for a "competition-type sports roadster," as Chrysler described the Falcon, were not to be fulfilled. According to Richard M. Langworth in his December 1985 story for *Car Collector,* "To Virgil Exner, the Chrysler Falcon was the big one that got away—the nearest he came to convincing Chrysler to build a Thunderbird."

The clay model shipped to Ghia was fairly close to the finished car.

Note the shape of the area surrounding the grille, the badging, and the shape of the hood. Also changed for the final car was the profile of the windshield.

The louvers on the final car, below, were not seen on the clay model.

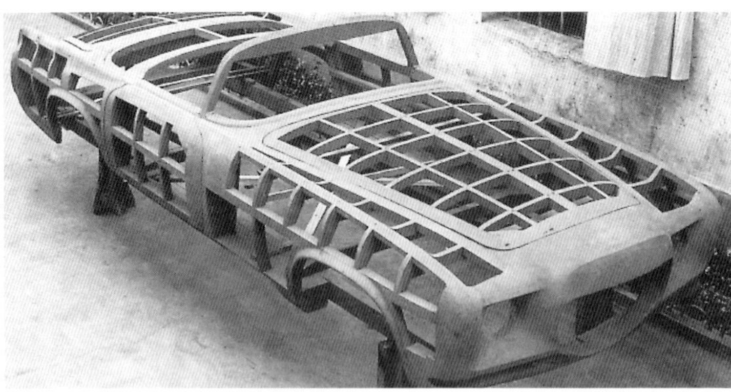

This is the Ghia-built wooden buck for the Falcon. According to Richard M. Langworth in the December 1985 issue of *Car Collector*, Ghia charged Chrysler only $20,000 to build all three Falcons.

Exner was now busy with production design, and the design of the Falcon was mostly the work of Maury Baldwin, who later said, "It was a crying shame they never produced that car." Exner believed that, produced in volume, the car could have been sold for the price of a Corvette.

The Falcon, a name chosen, according to Virgil Exner Jr., because of his father's love of dramatic birds, embodied many elements explored in previous idea cars. Here, for example, was a variation on the front-end treatment found in the K-310 series, complete with "pancake" hood and recessed headlights. However, tightly formed bumpers now split and folded down to expose the heart-shaped grille, which became taller in the translation from clay to steel. Also, above the grille there was a two-piece

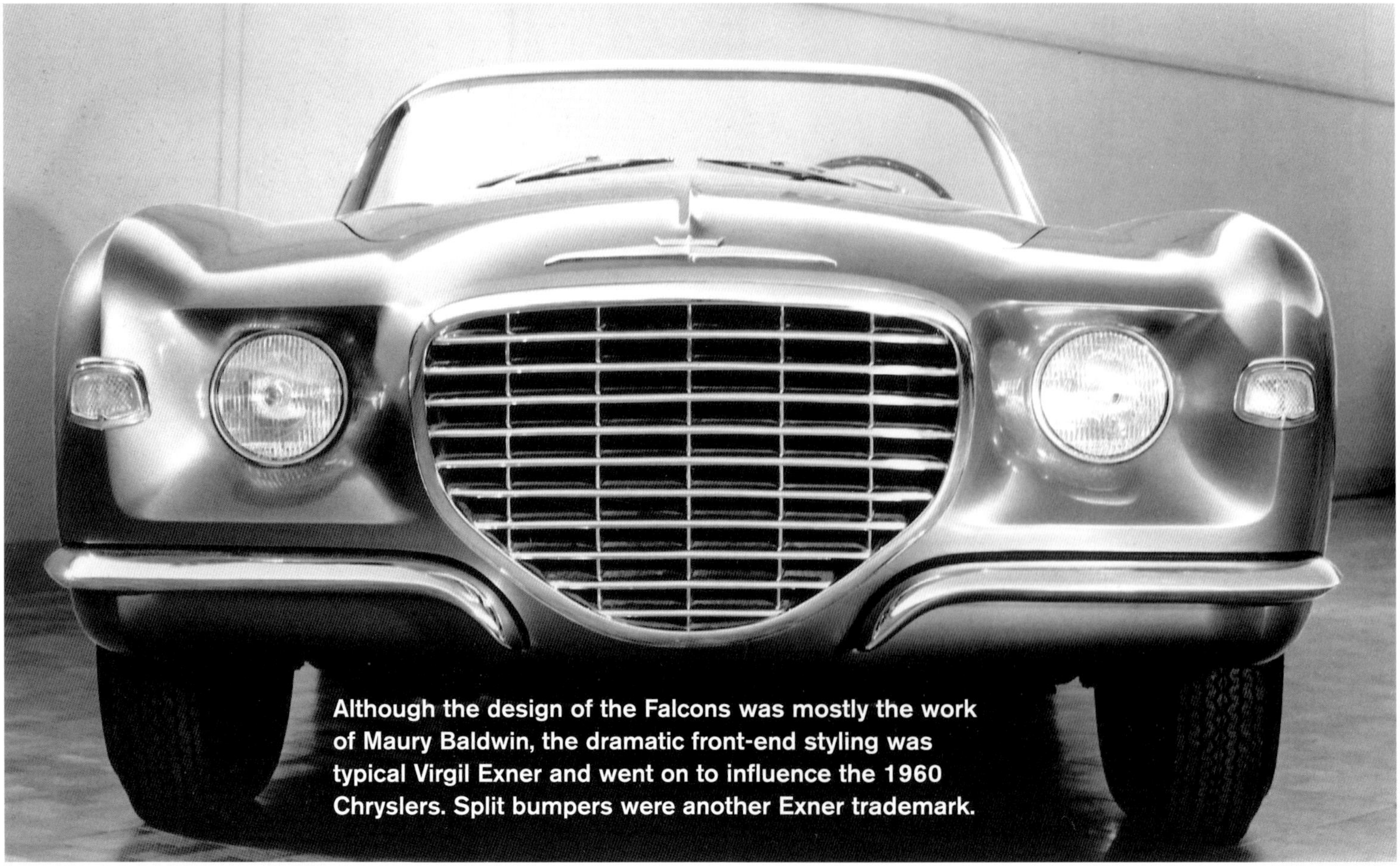

Although the design of the Falcons was mostly the work of Maury Baldwin, the dramatic front-end styling was typical Virgil Exner and went on to influence the 1960 Chryslers. Split bumpers were another Exner trademark.

Probably photographed in Italy, this Falcon was fitted with a different set of hubcaps from those shown in other photographs. In most instances, the Falcons were fitted with 15-inch chrome wire wheels. The white fabric top folded away into a storage compartment behind the seats.

chrome crown and wing emblem that was repeated on the decklid.

The fenders, in the front at least, were like those of the Firearrow series, as was the windshield and the convertible top, which again was stowed in a compartment behind the cockpit. There were also De Soto Adventurer-style functional side pipes, complete with heat shielding, under the doors. Heavily flared wheel openings likewise had the flavor of the De Soto, but the forward-facing side louvers (not seen in the clay models) were a departure.

Toward the rear the design moved away from its progenitors to an unusual treatment in which the wide tailfins with their simulated vents housing taillights ended in heavy, chromed vertical bumpers that rolled forward under the car. A center-mounted, floating bumper was not dissimilar from that first seen on the '53 SS. However, the gas filler was placed just above and to the left of the bumper. The decklid was push-button operated.

Like many early Exner/Baldwin collaborations, Falcons featured large wheels tightly filling the wheel wells. The tires were 7.60 x 15 wide white walls fitted to chrome wire wheels. Contemporary photographs of one black or navy blue Falcon show it with vented hubcaps and fake, two-eared spinners.

Mechanically, Falcons were based on 105-inch wheelbase production chassis, highly modified to accommodate the 276-ci 170-hp De Soto FireDome Hemi with single 2-barrel carburetor and PowerFlite transmission.

According to Richard M. Langworth who wrote about driving one of the Falcons in the December 1985 issue of *Car Collector*, "It had fine performance potential, though I didn't get to wring it out—partly because of its value, partly because of a curious in-line PowerFlite shifter which never seemed to find the right gear." Other technical highlights included Chrysler's new Coaxial Power Steering, power brakes, and electric window lifts.

The interiors of the three cars were mostly created by the Ghia studios, and they were both tasteful and very European. The process by which Chrysler contracted Ghia to build its cars was at least a communal evolution. Chrysler would supply Ghia with specifications, clays, and drawings, and Ghia's craftsmen would then create a fairly accurate version of what Chrysler had envisaged. Many changes occurred during this translation, but usually they were quite well-received. According to

Rear view was simplicity itself. Wide fins split by heavy chrome bumperettes contained taillights. Badging emulated that of the hood and the gas filler cap was mounted above and to the left of the floating bumper.

Langworth, Ghia charged Chrysler $20,000 to build the three Falcons.

The dash used aircraft-style slide control switching with large round, chromed bezelled gauges, wood-rim steering wheels, and leather bucket seats. To give either the black- or red-and-ivory interior more visual depth and wider shoulder room, the door panels were concaved to emphasize the deep cockpit interior. In his driving impressions, Langworth stated, "We also found the Falcon a tight fit for anybody over 5 feet 10 inches, and there wasn't any headroom." Of course, had the Falcon, which stood only 51.2 inches high, gone on to production, many elements—including the low roof height— might have been changed. Its overall length was 182 inches—the shortest of all the Chrysler idea cars—and it measured 68.3 inches wide.

According to Bruno Alfieri's history of Ghia, the Falcon was introduced alongside the two Flight Sweep idea cars "in the main hall of the Chrysler Building in New York during the Christmas holiday of 1955. It was an astounding success: In addition to the more than 85,000 VIPs invited by Chrysler over the ten days of the exhibition, it is estimated that at least one-and-a-half million New Yorkers admired the cars in the windows." Of course, the Falcon embodied completely different styling from the Flight Sweeps, which would introduce the "Forward Look."

Contemporary magazines indicate that one of the Falcons was painted red, another light blue, while the third car was either black or navy blue. They were favorites of Exner's, and he even brought one of the cars to Watkins Glen, where he paced the annual grand prix. Production, however, was to elude the design, and even the name was given to Ford when, according to the oral history of Virgil Exner Jr., "Henry Ford II very much wanted that name, and he went to Tex Colbert and asked if they could have the name. Tex asked my father if that was okay and he said, 'Well, I guess. They do us some favors once in a while, [and] we do them some favors, and so that's okay.'"

Although the Falcon did not attain production status, various design elements did translate into production models a few years later with the front-end treatments of the 1960 Chrysler New Yorker, Saratoga, and 300-F.

1955 *Flight Sweep I & II*

The Flight Sweep I and II idea cars of 1955 introduced Virgil Exner's "Forward Look" in advanced engineering and design. Created as non-identical twins, this coupe and convertible were full four-seaters, which were sporty in nature but not exotic in the European sense. They were built with American buyers in mind, using traditional Chrysler V-8 power, suspension, brakes, and steering on Chrysler production chassis. According to Richard M. Langworth writing in the December 1985 issue of *Car Collector*, "The Flight Sweep I (convertible) and II (coupe) were two more 1955 Maury Baldwin cars—Exner was by now busy with production design—and here we see the arrival of the fin along with the ever-prevalent toilet seat spare, soon to be a production car feature."

Both vehicles were debuted, along with the final Falcon, on August 16, 1955, in New York in the Chrysler International Salon, and they featured many new construction details, including smooth,

Flight Sweep I

This 3/8-scale clay model of the Flight Sweep photographed on April 6, 1954, gives a clear indication of the intended direction. It also shows how close the original concept was to the finished vehicles. The recessed, hooded headlamps are there, as is the trim that angles back sharply before turning upwards to delineate the fin—itself the shape of fins to come. However, the pronounced eyebrow over the windshield was eliminated.

THE *FORWARD* LOOK

"These 9 top aircraft designers salute
Chrysler Corporation's all-new 1955 styling."

L. L. Colbert, President

Left to Right: Alexander Kartveli, Republic Aviation Corp. • Michael Gluharoff, Sikorsky Aircraft Division, United Aircraft Corp. • Hall Hibbard, Lockheed Aircraft Corp. • Glenn L. Martin, Founder, Glenn L. Martin Co. • Louis Breguet, Société Ateliers d'Aviation • John K. Northrop, Founder, Northrop Aircraft Corp. • William T. Piper, Piper Aircraft Corp. • Robert J. Woods, Bell Aircraft Corp. • George Trimble, Jr., Glenn L. Martin Co.

THESE famous aircraft designers attended a preview of Chrysler Corporation's all-new concept of automotive style for 1955: THE FORWARD LOOK.

They saw new-styled engineering *...entirely new design* from frame to roof . . . created to match the mood of today's car owners.

They saw new length, new lowness. They sensed *motion* even when the cars were standing still.

They found new features the public has been seeking . . . features right up an air-minded man's alley.

They were right at home with the New-Horizon windshields—fully swept back and fully wrapped around—windshields that provide visibility equalled only by an airplane pilot's.

They noted the convenience of the PowerFlite Range Selector in a logical new place—a place an aircraft designer might have chosen.

THE FORWARD LOOK intrigued these men as it is bound to intrigue you, too. It brings together the things you have been asking for—in looks, in luxury, in comfort, in performance. It will bring you fresh pride of ownership every time you step into your 1955 Chrysler Corporation car.

Be sure to see THE FORWARD LOOK in the new Plymouth, Dodge, De Soto, Chrysler and Imperial cars for 1955.

The 1955 PLYMOUTH • DODGE • DE SOTO • CHRYSLER • IMPERIAL

CHRYSLER CORPORATION > THE *FORWARD* LOOK

Copyright 1954 Chrysler Corporation

Chrysler used nine eminent designers from the world of aviation to introduce and endorse the new "Forward Look."

With the top up or down, Flight Sweep I was perhaps more stylish than its hardtop sister car. The top-up shot was taken in Detroit. Flight Sweep I was painted Vapor White on the top and Solar Bronze below the trim line.

Photographed here in Italy before shipment to the United States, the convertible looks slightly out of place with its color-accentuated fins and the spare wheel "thrown" onto the decklid; there was no spare-wheel cover fitted. Notice also that here the car was fitted with chrome wire wheels, not the turbo vane hubcaps fitted later and copied by the aftermarket.

This rarely seen photograph of the wooden buck was taken at Ghia. The subsequent shape of the Flight Sweeps can be seen, even down to the shape of the taillights and the split rear bumpers.

clean body lines which were unbroken by seams or joints. Welding the front fenders, cowl, and body together and filling the joints achieved this seamless look.

Built, of course, by Ghia, the steel bodies were mounted on top of modified De Soto chassis with a wheelbase of 120 inches. Overall they measured 207 inches, and they sat seven inches lower than a production 1955 Plymouth, at 53 inches. They were actually three inches longer than a production 1955 Plymouth four-door sedan, and even with their low rooflines they still offered more than spacious comfort for four passengers.

Although there was an obvious family resemblance, their styling was quite a departure from previous idea cars. However, they gave more than a hint of what was soon to roll off production lines. For example, the front end featured headlamps recessed deep under the fender tops, predicting future production cars, the 1957 Imperial in particular. It was a feature Chrysler would employ for many years. A trim molding angled back sharply from the fender, sweeping all the way back to the rear quarter where it turned upwards to delineate the tail fin that extended above the natural fender line. The fin was just a hint of the excess to follow.

To match the "Forward Look" of the fenders, the grille was angled forward aggressively, and it predicted the shape of grilles as well as the egg-crate insert to come in the 1960 Chryslers. The split front bumper was another recurring theme, and here they contained direction indicators.

Moving rearward, there was a "clamshell-style" hood and a definite speedboat cowl anchoring a sharply sloping (56-degrees), wide-horizon windshield. The windshield was flanked by small, round rearview mirrors mounted to the long doors. The side glass was curved, which for 1955 was a nearly unheard-of detail.

The hardtop coupe had a very delicate roof with slim pillars—it was reminiscent of the Raymond Loewy-attributed '53 Studebaker—the C-pillar angling forward sharply. Uncharacteristically, slim vertical ribs bisected the rear glass.

The interior of the convertible was quite exciting, with its tapered steering column topped with a delicate three-spoke wheel. Large round instrument nacelles were spread across the dash. The center console swept up to the dash and contained the radio as well as left-to-right slider controls for the heater, turn signals, and the selector for the PowerFlite automatic transmission.

The counterbalanced decklid was split into two. The upper half contained the spare wheel cover, while the wheel was secured in the lower half for ease of access.

The split bumper theme was repeated in the rear, where there was also a locking gas cap and a rather intriguing two-piece, counterbalanced decklid. The shape of the spare wheel was pressed into the upper half of the decklid, which opened forward. The spare wheel itself was actually located in the lower half of the decklid, which opened rearwards so that the spare could be easily removed. Below the bumpers, which contained backup lights on either side of

the centrally mounted license plate, were a pair of "fish tail" exhaust outlets, each with vertical ribs.

Every design element of the Flight Sweeps emphasized the "Forward Look." Even the wheel openings and wheels were used to present the motion of speed with ribbed chassis shields inside the wheel wells. The wheel covers simulated sporty exposed brake drums and cooling fins, and the aftermarket quickly copied them. They were fitted to 7.10 x 15-inch white-wall tires.

Each car featured a different two-tone paint treatment. The top half of Flight Sweep I was finished in Vapor White and Solar Bronze on the sides. Flight Sweep II was finished in jet-black on the upper surfaces and Airfoil Green below the belt line molding.

The interior featured cockpit styling with a sweeping instrument panel that rolled out into the door panels. The dash was fitted with large circular instruments that included a tachometer and speedometer. There was also a combination switch for headlights, parking lights, and wipers. A second control panel was set into the console between the two front bucket seats, which featured air-foam cushions. This second panel housed slider controls for operating the heater and the turn signals. Controls for the PowerFlite transmission selec-

tor and the radio were also located in the console.

The rear seat was upholstered in the style of the front bucket and featured a large folding center armrest. Both cars were handled slightly differently in their upholstery. Flight Sweep I featured bronze and white leather throughout, while Flight Sweep II was trimmed in green and onyx leather. Both cars featured the extensive use of anodized aluminum trim throughout the interior.

While Flight Sweep II had a conventional steel roof, its convertible sibling used a spring counter-balanced convertible top mechanism that was easy to raise and lower by hand.

Power for both cars was supplied by 276-ci Chrysler Hemi V-8s, according to company press releases. With single 2-barrel carburetors and 7.5:1 compression ratio, they produced 170 hp at 4,400 rpm. Both cars were fitted with PowerFlite automatic transmissions.

Their steering wheels were delicate three-spoke items connected to the "Full-Time Coaxial Power" steering option. Chrysler's new Power Safety Brakes on both Flight Sweep models enhanced braking.

Exner's "Forward Look" was starting to pay dividends, and the ideas expressed in his idea cars were finally finding their way into production. And while the Flight Sweeps never saw production, their direct connection to Chrysler production vehicles of the time and the immediate future is obvious.

1956 *Chrysler Norseman*

There is no other idea car that has intrigued and fascinated Chrysler hobbyists and historians more than the Norseman. It was one of the most important projects the studios turned out in a hectic year of marvelous work. Bill Brownlie and Virgil Exner created a test bed for both engineering and styling, using a production Chrysler 129-inch wheelbase chassis with a mixture of steel and aluminum body panels, an advanced V-8, and a PowerFlite push-button automatic transmission.

Not only was the Norseman a radical departure in body form, it also showed great promise with innovative features. It had full underbody sheetmetal for smoothing out the air flow, many electrical innovations, and an intriguing roof with unconventional, very thin A pillars. Chrysler press releases at the time noted, "The Norseman incorporated more structural, chassis, electrical, and styling innovations than any other 'idea' car ever designed by Chrysler."

The structural innovation was its unique roof design, which was an enormous cantilevered fastback featuring massive, buttressed C-pillars, leaving an expansive, curved windshield as the only other supporting element. Exner was intrigued with the concept of creating an uninterrupted forward and side view for the driver of the Norseman. Although the cantilevered roof never reached production, the theme was partly used in some Chrysler products after 1956, including the Plymouth Fury, Dodge Coronet, the Chrysler New Yorker, and the 1966–67 Dodge Charger. These vehicles employed similar treatment with very thin A-pillars, and deeply curved and raked windshields.

In an interview conducted in July 2000, Dana Waterman, who worked for Cliff Voss in the advanced studio as a studio engineer, said, "The A pillar was nothing more than 1/8-inch steel rod with turnbuckles that tied the header to the cowl and clamped the windshield. There was no seal between the edge of the windshield and the door glass—but we hoped to find something suitable later on."

According to Virgil Exner Jr., in his Ford oral history, "The object behind this was safety, to a great extent. Not only from a vision standpoint, but from the fact that in a roll-over situation, it was thought that the rods would shear, and the roof would actually spring up, giving a crush-proof situation to the occupants."

Waterman went on to recall, "Jack Charipar called the frame the 'Savonuzzi sandwich,' because Giovanni had designed it. It consisted of cross-formed webs sandwiched between thick steel plates. It ran between the toe board and the rear kickup where the roof pillars were fastened. Of course, we never had the chance to test it."

The body surfaces were massaged by Jerry Schnoor, and due to the sweeping fastback, the height of the trunk space was cut in half as it rolled directly down to the oval-shaped freestanding rear bumper. The bumper sat on a deeply sculptured center section set between a pair of oval-section rear fenders complete with fins on the tops and

According to Ghia historian David Burgess-Wise, Ghia spent 15 months and 45 million lira building the Norseman.

sides. The end of the driver's side fin contained a flip-open fuel door. The fenders were capped with heavily chromed, combination vertical bumperettes and taillight assemblies.

Another roof innovation was a powered, 12-square-foot sliding rear glass that moved forward into the roof panel, exposing the rear parcel shelf and part of the rear seat. The C-pillar was sculptured with a secondary form that reflected the same sweeping lines of the roof, window opening, and the deeply sculptured wheel arches. The inside of the wheel arches was highlighted with a touch of red.

The body was painted two-tone metallic green split at the belt line with a chrome spear, creating a smart look that was traditional for Chrysler's products of the time. There were no door handles, just push buttons, to open the doors.

The front end was also unique, with hidden headlights fitted into the tops of the front fenders, a combination grille and bumper with rounded protruding park and turn signals, and a front-hinged hood. True to the concept-to-production-line practice of the design studio, the fender shapes were passed on to the '57 Imperial. The hidden headlights appeared the following year on the Imperial D'Elegance, but then disappeared until they resurfaced 10 years later on the '68 Chrysler 300.

Under the hood was a 331-ci "polyspheric" V-8, to quote Chrysler's literature. With a single 4-barrel carburetor, it was rated at 235 hp at 4,400 rpm.

The interior was designed by Deo Lewton and featured four power-operated bucket seats. The backs of the front seats were designed to pivot to the center of the car, allowing for easier access to the rear seat. The Norseman was also one of the first cars to use lap seat belts, which retracted into housings in the center console and doors. The seats were described by Chrysler as trimmed in "green-and-gray metallic leather." Bill Brownlie designed the instrument panel.

The Norseman was built at Ghia in about 15 months as a

The rear window retracted into the roof. Fenders featured vertical and horizontal fins, with a fuel door at the end of the driver's side.

fully functional aluminum-bodied automobile. Unfortunately, it was more than a month late and left Genoa, Italy, on July 17, 1956, aboard the ill-fated Italian passenger liner SS *Andrea Doria*. There was such a rush to ship the car that only a few photographs were taken.

The *Andrea Doria* had sailed the Atlantic for several years carrying passengers and cargo between Italian and European ports and the East Coast of the United States. On July 25, the day before she was due to arrive in New York, the *Andrea Doria* collided with the Swedish–American liner *Stockholm* in thick fog off the Massachusetts coast 50 miles south of Nantucket. The Italian captain's last desperate maneuver put his ship broadside to the *Stockholm*'s ice-breaking prow, which sliced directly into the *Andrea Doria*'s garage area, where the Norseman was stowed. Of the 1,706 people aboard, 1,660 were rescued. But on July 26, three days after Exner suffered a near-fatal heart attack resulting in open-heart surgery, the ship sank 225 feet to the bottom of the ocean. According to Exner Jr., his father thought, "That's neat, one of my cars went down in a big famous shipwreck."

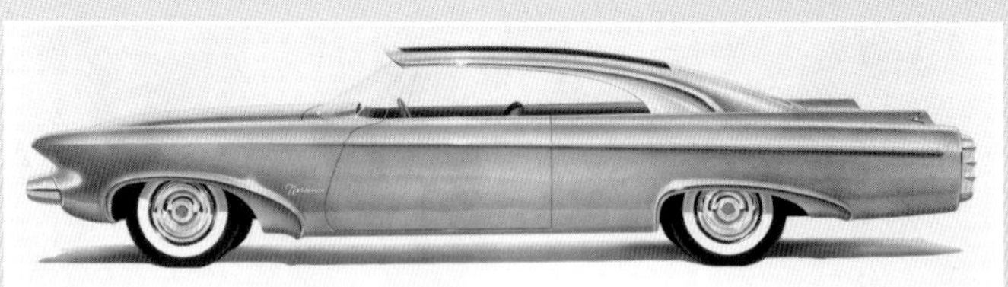

Norseman Sketch

This sketch of the Norseman, so-named apparently because of Exner's Norwegian heritage, was the work of Deo Lewton, according to designer Thom Taylor, who worked with Lewton at International Harvester in the 1970s. The Norseman was the first Chrysler-Ghia collaboration built entirely from engineering drawings. Previously, Ghia had been shipped clay models, but engineering vice president James C. Zeder and chief body engineer H.E. Chesebrough sought control of Ghia's processes. The interference did not sit well with Ghia or with Virgil Exner; nevertheless, he and Chrysler Styling Chief Cliff Voss handed the project to Bill Brownlie in 1954. The project was developed in his Imperial studio into 1955. The scale model never left Highland Park, Michigan, but Ghia's translation was exemplary. The Norseman was the second longest of Chrysler's idea cars, measuring 227.5 inches overall. It was also the widest vehicle at 82 inches, and it stood 56 inches tall.

Rarely seen interior photograph clearly shows the Bill Brownlie-designed instrument panel with two wide-set round gauges. The rest of the interior Brownlie credited to Deo Lewton. It featured green-and-gray metallic leather-covered bucket seats with lap belts that retracted into the seats and the transmission tunnel. All four seats were electronically adjustable—the fronts in such a way, and by remote control if necessary, as to allow ingress and egress to the rear.

1956 *Plymouth Plainsman*

The first of several station wagon idea cars was the eight-passenger Plymouth Plainsman introduced on January 7, 1956, at the Chicago Auto Show.

According to Bill Robinson, "Dave Scott of the Plymouth Studio designed the Plainsman in 3/8-scale. Production studios weren't manned for show car development, but they were allowed to do a few models to keep the juices flowing. Selected models were then sent to Maury Baldwin's Styling Research Studio for full-scale completion."

Looking to the American West for inspiration, Maury Baldwin finished Scott's Plainsman in metallic Palomino Beige, with a white-fabric-padded top on the outside and natural calf hide and leather inside. Gold Texas Longhorn medallions adorned the B-pillars and tailgate. Baldwin predicted the wagon, an expression of Chrysler's "Flight Sweep" theme, might reach production.

The roof of the Plainsman was described as "stepped and cantilevered." It also had air intakes in the leading edge. However, the angle of the B-pillar made ingress and egress difficult for the center-row passengers.

Behind the full-length fender skirt on the passenger side was the concealed spare, raised and lowered with a mechanical crank.

The front seats folded out of the way to allow access to the center row. All were covered in a combination of natural calf hide and natural leather.

While production would not figure in the Plainsman's future, many of its design ideas would. For example, its "Observation Car" rear-facing third seat; the remote-controlled, electrically operated tailgate and rear window lift; the spare tire mounted inside the right rear fender; the white vinyl-trimmed roof; and a roof with steps and a rack would all figure in future production automobiles. In fact, the third seat had been a standard feature in 1930s and 1940s woody station wagons, but they had all been forward-facing. The electrically operated, folding, rear-facing rear seat was a brand new idea. Also, the center row of seats could likewise be folded to form a large flat cargo deck—a feature found on most of today's wagons. Contemporary press releases said, "The entire interior of the car can be transformed at will into one vast double bed!" Meanwhile, the front seats had fully adjustable seat backs to ease ingress and egress to the center seats.

The Plainsman's lines were very much in keeping with contemporary styling, with rounded body sheetmetal, low-profile tailfins—the left-hand fin concealing the gas filler cap—and integrated bumpers. The rear bumper also contained hydraulically operated, retractable steps to facilitate access to the third seat.

Of its many features, perhaps the Plainsman's most unique was its roof, described in the March 1956 issue of *Motor Trend* as, "both stepped and cantilevered." Chrome rails tied the front portion of the roof to the stepped-up rear, the leading edge of which contained vents for ducting air towards the rear seats. The angle of the wide B-pillar continued down into the doors that were consequently rather oddly shaped, making access to the center row of seats rather difficult.

Other features of the body included deeply hooded headlights, with the horizontal trim of their nacelles matching the bars of the split grille. Below each headlamp were large chrome fake-turbine intakes mounted at either end of the thick chrome bumper. A character line swept back from the bumper ends through the door to become the hinge line of the full-length fender skirts, with the passenger side housing the spare wheel. A hand-operated mechanical crank lowered and raised the spare, making it easier to change wheels.

As usual, Ghia built the body, this time atop a production 115-inch wheelbase Plymouth chassis fitted with 7.10 x 15-inch wheels, chrome hubcaps, and wide whitewall tires. Overall, the wagon measured 208 inches. It was 79.4 inches wide and stood 60.2 inches tall—the tallest of all the idea cars. Chrysler historical papers state that the Plainsman was powered by a 260-ci Red Ram V-8 (odd for a Plymouth-branded vehicle) fitted with a single 2-barrel carburetor. It produced 167 hp at 4,400 rpm. A PowerFlite automatic transmission was used.

Once the Plainsman concept car had done its duty at Chrysler, it was sold to a company employee who shipped it to Australia. Eventually, however, it was brought back to the United States.

The tailgate, the rear window, and the rear seat were all electrically operated and when folded flat offered an easily accessible cargo space.

1956 *Chrysler Dart*

The Dart measured 223 inches long, with a wheelbase of 129 inches and a height of 54 inches. The sleek lines allowed room for four—just.

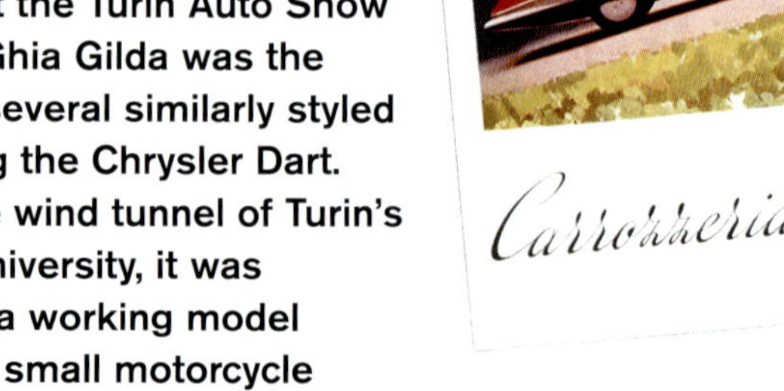

First shown at the Turin Auto Show of 1955, the Ghia Gilda was the precursor of several similarly styled cars, including the Chrysler Dart. Shaped in the wind tunnel of Turin's Politecnico University, it was reported that a working model powered by a small motorcycle engine, perhaps Count Lurani's 350-cc Moto Guzzi "Nibbio II," turned 125 mph. According to *Motor Life*, "Experts theorize that it could hit over 180 with a standard U.S. V-8, 225 mph in racing form."

When the Chrysler Dart appeared in the United States at the end of 1956, it was a truly radical departure from anything that had yet materialized from Chrysler. However, it wasn't the first of its kind, as Ghia had been experimenting with similar aerodynamic shapes for some time.

Ghia's Luigi Segre and Dr. Giovanni Savonuzzi had been conducting wind tunnel tests at the Turin Politecnico with a series of aerodynamic "mules." These tests led to their first full-size styling mockup, the non-running Gilda, which, according to Griff Borgeson in the February 1958 issue of *Motor Life*, "first saw the light of publicity in 1955, when photos of the Ghia Gilda appeared in the international press."

The shape obviously worked, for it was soon translated into running vehicles. For example, there was the Moto-Guzzi-powered single seater "Nibbio II" bodied by Ghia for Count Lurani's assault on the 350-cc class record. There was also an Alfa Romeo on an experimental SS-3500 chassis. And then at the Turin Auto Show in

The Dart was primarily aluminum-bodied, with steel doors and roof. Note the wraparound trim is already formed in the photo at far left.

the fall of 1955 there was a production prototype, the Chrysler Dart.

Though much bigger than the Gilda, the Dart, sometimes called the "Super Gilda," was built on a 129-inch, A-498 Imperial-size chassis and was powered by a 392-ci K300 Chrysler engine producing 375 hp at 5,200 rpm. It was fitted with the new TorqueFlite transmission.

What was significant about the Dart was that it had a drag coefficient of just 0.17. "Truly exceptional for such a car!" said Borgeson. The Dart's coefficient was less even than the radical Bertone BAT 5 (0.19). According to company vice president of engineering Paul Ackerman, "The Dart is the most perfect aerodynamic passenger car design in the world today. Its aerodynamic purity gives it less than one-third the air drag of any other passenger car yet built."

Apparently, during collaboration between Exner's design team, (including his number-one assistant, William Schmidt), Ghia, and Ackerman, some aspects of the Dart's design were simple variations of concepts already tried; others were original ideas. The Dart was, however, not just a simple show car but also an important research tool used by engineering at the Chelsea Proving Grounds.

The results of the wind tunnel testing conducted in Italy gave birth to the large vertical tail fins that stabilized the Dart at high speeds. Their shape also lowered the coefficient of drag by two-thirds of what was considered normal on 1956 production cars. Even though the Dart fin design never saw production, some Chrysler advertising featured a profile image showing how similar the tail of Art Tarabusi's USAF Saber Jet fighter was to the rear fin on Frank Bianchi's '56 Plymouth Fury. Both of these reserve pilots were then working as designers at Chrysler and helped put the ad together. Also, Chrysler vehicles in 1957, 1958, and 1959 all featured large vertical tail fins.

Primarily, the Dart was a 2+2 coupe, but an intricate retracting hardtop afforded multiple options: A section could be slid back like a sunroof; the whole roof could be partly retracted creating a landau effect; or the whole roof could be retracted into the trunk, turning the car into a full convertible—all while in motion. Even with the top down, luggage space was available.

Chrysler Dart instrumentation was clustered behind the steering wheel. Note the slider controls to the right.

The three-position, electrically operated steel top offered sunroof, landau, and convertible options. And, it could be operated while in motion.

Another unique feature in the Dart's body, which was primarily aluminum but with steel doors and roof, was its steeply raked windshield, which was set high into the roofline. Like the other 1956 prototypes, its A-pillars were extremely thin. However, Proving Ground test drivers complained that because of the low nose, they couldn't see where the front of the car was. Also, the size of the grille opening was refined to balance out the lift created by the air flowing through the grille into the engine compartment.

Chrome trim was used sparingly, which was typical of Virgil Exner, but what the car lacked in the way of trim it made up for with a wide body-encircling chrome

At Chrysler's Chelsea Proving Grounds, the Dart acquitted itself well. Its torsion-bar front suspension allowed the wheels to be tucked well inside the skirted fenders.

bumper that was fully isolated with an impact-absorbing rubber substructure.

The second longest idea car to date, the Dart measured 223 inches overall. It was 80 inches wide and stood 54 inches tall. It rode on 8.00 x 15-inch wheels. The finned wheel covers were said to force brake-cooling air at the rate of 80-cubic-feet per minute.

Interestingly, the Dart was scheduled to be shipped aboard the ill-fated *Andrea Doria* along with the Norseman, but last-minute work delayed the Dart's shipment for another month.

After 85,000 miles of track testing, Exner decided to get some more mileage out of it by revising the styling to give it a more production look. The Dart went back to Ghia in Italy, where it was rebodied and modified into the Dart Diablo. The tailfins were shrunk, and a more production-like windshield was installed with a conventional folding soft top. It was repainted in Diablo Red and re-introduced in January 1958 at the Chicago Auto Show, trimmed with three-pronged spears on the rear fenders and very fine chrome door handles.

The whole Dart/Dart Diablo project had cost only $250,000, and the return was seen as a highly effective method of creating fully functional concept cars that were tough enough to withstand the rigors of real road testing—much the same as Chrysler did in the 1990s.

Because of Ghia's involvement in the project, Chrysler sold the Diablo back to Ghia in July 1958. Ghia initially used the Diablo for their own corporate displays, but after passing through numerous owners, it eventually worked its way back to the United States.

Dual Ghia—Again

In 1958, Gene Casaroll of Automobile Shippers, Inc. and Dual-Ghia fame tried once again to ignite the public's interest in a Chrysler-platformed, Ghia-bodied production car. Working as he had previously with Paul Faragoe, who not only managed Dual Motors' custom automotive department but was also Ghia's U.S. representative, they based the new model on the 300-D and the Chrysler Dart.

As with the previous 1956–57 model, chassis shipped in from Chrysler were prepared and shipped to Italy, where Ghia built up the steel body and installed the trim and interiors. Back in Detroit, a dozen or so men worked on a miniature assembly line—the vehicles mounted on rolling racks—to install engines and complete the assembly.

While they retained the essence of the Dart's styling, many changes were made to simplify the design for limited production, and the retractable roof went away. A scoop now appeared on the hood, and the elegant grille gave way to chrome vertical bars. No doubt to ease production, many existing Chrysler parts, such as the taillights, fuel filler cap, door handles, and windshield were used. The dash was also from the 300-D, but a record player and radio were stacked upon the transmission tunnel. Bucket seats were upholstered in two-tone leather to match the exterior, which on the prototype was black and saffron yellow.

As to the price, well, at the time *Motor Life* wrote about it in its October 1958 issue, they guessed, "Somewhere in the neighborhood of $12,000."

Imperial D'Elegance

According to the Oct.–Nov. 1972 issue of *Special Interest Autos* magazine, "[Virgil] Exner never liked [the] 1958 Imperial D'Elegance pillar-less fastback. It had several different designers who could never agree on the overall look." That may well be true, for the D'Elegance was an ungainly concept that reflected the confusion of the end of the fin era and the search for a new direction. Why then would it warrant so much space in this book? Because when one looks carefully one can clearly see the collision of past and future.

A rendering of what was obviously designated to be a 300—evidence the logo on the door. However, little of this elegant design would eventually translate to production, save perhaps the profile of the fins.

This 3/8-scale model was developed and it displayed many of the design cues of the rendering. The front end remained much the same, though the grille had vertical rather than horizontal bars. Also, some of the details were changed and the inset window was added.

The 3/8-scale model of John Pinko was, according to Dana Waterman, "Used as a visual reference. John had joined Chrysler from Ford. He worked in Maury Baldwin's Advanced Studio at Outer Drive in the late-1950s. He left and went to Peugeot in France but returned to work for Dick Macadam and Don DeLaRossa, dreaming up special things to do with the K-car."

According to Robert Ackerstet, author of *Chrysler 300: America's Original Musclecar*, these photographs of design #613 were dated October 10, 1955. They clearly show the genesis of the design of the prototype and production 1957 300C—particularly the grille.

Unfortunately, few of these photographs were dated, so it is rather difficult to put everything in chronological order. Nevertheless, the tale begins with the side elevation pictured in this chapter, which probably dates from the early- to mid-1950s, for it had definite traces of the ill-fated Norseman. For example, the profile of the front end was very similar. Though differing in details, they had similar covered headlamp treatments, and the shape of the fender predicted Exner's "Forward Look."

There was a speedboat cowl, wrap-over and wrap-around windshield, and curved side glass cut high into the roof and flush to the doors. The roof itself was cantilevered—there being no visible A-pillars—with a wide C-pillar. Note also the lightened central roof brace that curved gracefully down to the decklid. Moving further back, the fins, complete with 300 nomenclature, evolved from the D'Elegance character line halfway up the door and well ahead of the jamb, and swept up and back into what could have been the largest fins Chrysler ever produced—had the design gone into production.

The Deo Lewton rendering was obviously translated into a 3/8-scale model created by Cliff Voss and completed with "John Pinko" for proportioning. The scale model faithfully followed the rendering except in minor details. According to studio engineer Dana Waterman, "The curved side glass rolling over into the roof could not retract into the door, so the little drop-window inset had to be added for access." That feature would appear on later Chrysler concepts, including the Portofino. Close inspection reveals that glass panels were also to have been let into the roof above the front seats and that the backlight was split.

Other differences between the rendering and the clay model are evident in the detailing of the grille, and the size and location of the lower lamps. The character line in the side was remarkably similar, but the details differed. The flutes connecting the front fenders and doors were gone, the 300 insignia on the back of the door was replaced with louvers, and the large round insignia on the fenders was replaced with a circular EXP-15 logo.

While the EXP-15 model would not itself be translated into a full-size clay—as far as we know—elements of its design were incorporated into at least two subsequent vehicles, including a prototype for the '57 300C and the subsequent D'Elegance show car.

According to Robert Ackerson in his book *Chrysler 300*, published by Veloce, the clay styling model number 613, which became the prototype 300C of 1957, was photographed on October 10, 1955, and it clearly predicted both the front end styling of the 300C prototype and the production '57 300C.

In most surviving photographs the car has a license plate that read 1957 C-300-C but in the photograph to the right, the car wears a conventional plate, suggesting that it was used for some road testing and evaluation. The rear fenders and the greenhouse cetainly found a home on the '57 Plymouth.

For example, with single rather than dual headlamps and minus the large cross-form molding bisecting the grille, the front end of number 613 was a clear indicator of both the prototype and production '57 300C (albeit modified, the cross-form molding did eventually find a home on the front of the '60 300F). The chrome-trimmed eyebrows encircling the headlamps made it to both vehicles, as did the signature Exner-shaped grille. However, it was the prototype's egg-crate insert rather than the clay model's that went on the production car. The intakes under the headlamps and the bumper form translated to the prototype, but the bumper, while its shape remained, took on a new lower section as well as side marker lights.

The central hood fin did not live beyond the prototype.

Moving rearward, the character line that ran under the headlamp nacelle and flowed beautifully into the fenderwell made it, as did the windshield with its protruding upper frame. Ackerman conceded that, "The 'spoiler' over the windshield was a feature that had a negative impact on the coupe's top-speed potential." The air duct in the clay made it to the prototype but not to production. Likewise, the greenhouse was simplified dramatically. A large scoop mounted low in the rear quarter that did not make it to production was featured on the prototype. From that point rearward the prototype closely resembled the clay, with its large fins that incorporated

The prototype '57 300C sits outside an engineering building. Although fabricated in steel by Ghia, it was neither show car nor conventional prototype, nor was it ever shown publicly. However, features of the design did make it to production. For example, the front end was very close to the production '57 300C, although that car would have dual rather than single headlamps.

taillight moldings and bumperettes. They flanked a large, chrome-trimmed spare wheel assembly—complete with tri-bar spinner—that appeared to float behind the car.

According to DaimlerChrysler design manager Jeff Godshall, "What the 300C prototype does look like, however, is the special one-off '55 Imperial convertible that was built for Chrysler chairman K.T. Keller."

The spare was flanked by cast exhaust outlets, which in some photographs appear to be functional only on the passenger side. In other photographs, both outer slots appear functional. Above the driver's side outlet was an asymmetrically mounted, recessed license plate. None of these details were transferred to the production 300C. In fact,

the rear end of the production vehicle was atypically clean. In a modified form, however, the rear fenders did find a home on the '57 Plymouth, as did the greenhouse shared with Dodge.

According to Ghia historian David Burgess-Wise, Ghia built a full-size steel prototype from the clay, which was photographed at Ghia before being shipped to Detroit, where it was probably turned into a running car. Most photographs show it with a show license plate saying 1957 C-300-C; some shots show it with a conventional plate, indicating it was probably evaluated, though Dana Waterman remembered, "It was a steel car, but I don't know if it ever ran. When I saw the body during buildup it was black, and may have had a silver roof. I don't believe it was ever shown."

What was shown, in 1958, was the evolution of the EXP-15, the Imperial D'Elegance. Built upon an 129-inch

Tall, canted fins flanked a rather neat fastback decklid complete with trunk. The gunsights atop the rear lights looked out of place, as did the vertical bars added to the split bumpers. Virgil Exner was not a fan of Cliff Voss's evolution of the EXP-15.

The non-functional D'Elegance was the longest of its contemporaries measuring 228 inches overall. It rode on an 129-inch wheelbase chassis. The front wheelwells were extreme but some design cues such as the fins and the fastback feature were to be found on the production 1957 Plymouth Fury and later C-bodies.

wheelbase—as long as any Chrysler show car of its era—the four-door D'Elegance belied its name and stretched to a record length—for company show car—of 228 inches. It measured 79.3 inches wide and was 52.3 inches tall. It was a mock-up only, so there was no running gear, but it rode on wide 9.50 x 14-inch tires mounted on steel wheels with chrome hubcaps.

The front end, with the exception of its trim and the bumper details, translated verbatim from the EXP-15. The headlamps were hidden behind rotating covers. However, trim that peaked into small windsplits in the centers of the fenders flowed away down the side—bisecting the full-fender skirts—all the way to the rear bumper. In doing so, it visually chopped the car into sections that didn't seem to work well together.

The full-width integral bumper treatment with horizontal bars, similar to some tried on pre-production prototype '57 300s, was well executed. To the rear were exposed fender wells, while above was the EXP-15's speedboat cowl and large wraparound/wrap-over windshield, and, while the side glass was very flush to the metal, it did not extend up into the roof.

Unfortunately, no photographs could be found with the doors open. It would have been interesting to see how the B-pillar supporting the front-hinged rear doors

was constructed. All the side glass had lightweight chrome frames, and all retracted fully, including the rear side glass. The backlight was somewhat conventional, though the decklid flowed gently in fastback style to the rear and contained a trunk.

The fins, which blossomed out of the rear doors, were tall and angled outward, and they somewhat resembled those of the '57 Plymouth Fury. At their base were small, round gun sights atop large, round taillights. The bumpers, which featured three vertical bars, were split and flanked a chrome license plate frame.

Painted metallic blue with a richly detailed interior trimmed in cloth and leather, the D'Elegance was photographed in Detroit on September 10, 1958, and close inspection shows that the conventional round steering wheel seen through the windshield in the photograph taken at Ghia had been changed to a rectangular wheel with rounded corners.

The D'Elegance received scant press. However, it was used to illustrate several "Forecast from Detroit"-type articles, such as the one in *Motor Trend* that said, "This elegant variation on the Chrysler and Imperial theme is one of those design exercises that bears a strong enough resemblance to past styling trends to make its advances sound probabilities for the future."

1958 *Plmouth Cabana*

The Plymouth Plainsman was such a hit that the Plymouth Cabana quickly followed it, which, unlike the Plainsman, was a subdued styling mock-up, only with no running gear. Once again, the design was the work of Maury Baldwin, and it offered many innovative ideas with its crisp, clean modern looks.

In profile, the Cabana was rather pleasing. However, it had some quirky features, such as the front fenders that were coved in the front and protruded in the rear. The cowl had a hint of Virgil Exner's beloved speedboat profile, while the windshield wrapped both around and over. There was no B-pillar, and both doors opened from the center. There was a large sliding sunroof above the front passengers. Nevertheless, the top did make it to production on the '60 New Yorker wagon.

Only the driver's seat is visible in this photo. Either the other seats were added later or they all folded flat, which is unlikely.

was 80 inches wide and measured 55.9 inches tall. It rode on 8.00 x 14-inch medium-width whitewall tires.

Unfortunately, no photographs appear to have survived of the Cabana's most dramatic and unique feature: its center-opening doors with an innovative locking mechanism that eliminated the need for B-pillars. This feature, defined for the first time by Chrysler on the Cabana, has been explored time and again on subsequent Chrysler concepts, and as recently as on the Super 8 Hemi of 2001. However, it has never seen production at Chrysler.

The Cabana differed greatly from its predecessor, the Plainsman, in that it was far less gimmicky. There were, however, some odd touches, including a concave grille and quad freestanding headlights, which would appear on the 1961 Imperial. The Cabana also had very strange front wheel wells that were coved in the front yet flared out in the rear. They also had large flat areas that juxtaposed with the curvaceous body. The rear bumper was likewise concaved.

The roof treatment was also unique. Above the power-operated tailgate that opened to the driver's side, a pair of small skylights slid back into the roof when access to the third, rear-facing seat was required. There was also a steel-paneled sunroof over the front compartment. The rear-quarter glass was also very dramatic with heavy compound curvature. Incidentally, the two rear rows of seats could be folded flat into an expansive cargo deck. Early photographs show the car with what appears to be a separate driver's seat alongside a partial front bench seat—the first 30/70 front seat.

Like the exterior, the dash was simple and functional with the instruments housed in a beak-like binnacle mounted behind the steering wheel.

It's not known what happened to the Cabana. Most likely it was destroyed.

The tailgate opened to the side while the roof glass retracted into the roof. Third seat was rear-facing and could be folded flat along the center seat.

Maury was given three guidelines to follow: Create a multi-purpose domestic/commercial wagon (for example, an ambulance or a hearse); combine all the desirable features of station wagons into one wagon; and style it elegantly. This was no simple task given the various needs of an ambulance compared to a hearse. Nevertheless, Baldwin's design was both evolutionary and inventive, and many elements were later employed on both Chrysler and other Detroit-built production cars.

Built by Ghia on a 124-inch wheelbase production chassis, the Cabana measured 215.8 inches nose to tail. It

1959 DeSoto Cella I

Chrysler's long-term interest in an alternative to the internal combustion engine was primarily centered around the turbine engine, but other ideas were also seriously examined. One such concept was the fuel cell, and it was embodied in the De Soto Cella I.

The model was designed by Jack Kenitz in Maury Baldwin's Styling Research Studio. However, the project was handled by Chrysler's De Soto chief engineer A.E. Kimberly and featured an innovative electrochemical drive system which, for the time, was a radical departure from conventional drive systems. A forerunner of today's fuel cell cars, Cella I used energy created by a chemical reaction that produces hydrogen and oxygen. These gases would be fed into the fuel cell that produced electricity. The electricity was then used to power four electric engines. The system also incorporated lightweight reserve batteries, which were partly recharged via regenerative braking. According to Kimberly, "The system used much the same theory as a gas-powered engine uses gasoline, with the oxygen and hydrogen stored until they were required. These gases could be fed into the fuel cell so electricity could be generated instantaneously.

"The drive system would use four lightweight high-speed geared motors, one fitted to each wheel controlled by differential speed governors, and with the inherent high torque of this type of drive would provide excellent low-speed performance."

The Cella I was more of a design exercise than anything else, but it involved the development of multifaceted engineering and the marrying of technologies to create a nonworking model.

The body styling was dramatic, with aviation-styled tailfins flowing back from the front fenders and coved front wheel wells with an aerodynamically efficient body. The

A.E. Kimberly stands proudly behind the model of the Cella I. Four high-speed electric motors were to be positioned adjacent to the wheels, where they would drive through short, universal-jointed shafts to independently suspended shafts, eliminating transmission, differential, driveshaft, and rear axle.

hood was heavily louvered, and the split grille was a complete departure from traditional Chrysler styling. For example, so the roof could be built with greater structural integrity, there was no rear window. A periscope in the roof provided rearward vision.

Inside, Kimberly proposed that the Cella I would feature one of the first collapsible steering columns with a safety-padded dash panel, swivel front seats, rear-facing back seats, seat belts, and heated glass to eliminate frosting and fogging. Other proposed interior touches included a refrigerated cooler in the rear compartment, a swing-into-position television, a stereo sound system complete with a tape recorder, and a library of music. There was also to be built-in luggage fitted between the seats.

Unfortunately, the car never progressed past a 3/8-scale model, which was first shown at the Chicago Auto Show in 1959. The model was then toured extensively around the auto show scene in 1959, providing the public with a fascinating view of the future at the end of the 1950s. Many of its advanced ideas, which at the time were not viable concepts, have finally made production status 40 years later, proving the value of such "conceptive thought."

1960 *Plymouth XNR*

"I've never seen anything like it," said Harry E. Chesebrough, vice president of Chrysler and general manager of Plymouth. "We asked [Virgil] Exner to show the Chrysler Board of Management what could be done with a Plymouth of the future which would be a highly personalized car."

And show them he did.

A derivation of his name, the XNR was built by Ghia on a modified 106.5-inch Valiant chassis, and was powered by the new aluminum-block, 170-ci "Slant" 6-cylinder engine and a three-speed manual transmission. Initial testing gave 146 mph with the "Hyperpak" tuned manifold and 4-barrel carburetor. About 145 hp was available with the special cam and twin tuned exhausts. It was not fast enough for Exner.

Overall, the XNR measured 195.2 inches, 71 inches wide, and it stood just 46 inches tall. However, its most unusual feature was its asymmetrical styling with race car overtones in its headrest, which flared back into a stabilizer fin. The fin culminated in a bold chrome asymmetric cross—a striking design of the intersection of bumper blade and fin. Viewed from the rear it had the flavor of a Mondrian painting, using bold lines to achieve a startling new effect in automobile design. Exner said of the design, "With the XNR I was striving to avoid a static and bulky look. The goal was to create a graceful form with a built-in feeling of motion. The wedge shape expresses the function of automobiles because it imparts a sense of direction."

Studio engineer Dick Burke remembers, "I asked Ex about the shape of the XNR, particularly the wheel wells and the theme in the side which ended up on the Valiant, and he showed me pictures of various race cars he liked

Radiused rear wheel wells were another racecar-inspired design element, along with the competition-style cockpit, steel tonneau cover, and Brooklands-type passenger screen.

and how he had incorporated certain themes into his design."

The front-end treatment incorporated both the bumper and the grille into one element, a concept that eventually went into production, but it would be 11 years before it appeared on the Plymouth Satellite, Road Runner, and GTX in 1971. Dual headlights were mounted in the mesh. In the hood was an air scoop, complete with

In this shot of the car being unloaded, you can clearly see the asymmetrical X-form bumper. The car was bought by a meat wholesaler from Geneva, Switzerland, before being sold to the Shah of Persia (Iran).

XNR logo, that flared back into the cowl and over which the driver's windshield was formed. The passenger had a fold-down Brooklands-type windshield. For high-speed testing, the passenger compartment could be covered with a steel tonneau cover. The offset decklid featured a large, circular gas filler complete with XNR logo.

When testing of the XNR began, it was soon realized that 145 hp was just not enough, as Dick Burke remembered. "Exner wanted to go 150 mph, but the best it could do was 146 or -7 mph. He asked me what we could do. There wasn't much room under the hood for a supercharger or a turbo, so I asked for a free hand to design a fiberglass nose cone. There was no opportunity to test it in the wind tunnel, so I built a "shark nose" mouth below the nose cone and installed a bigger, shrouded radiator with two electric fans. The car was then taken to the Chelsea Proving Grounds where a professional driver went about 153 or 154 mph." Exner also took a turn behind the wheel and managed a creditable 143 mph.

Trimmed with a black leather interior and painted brilliant red, the XNR rode on custom 14-inch wheels fitted with special tires trimmed with slender one-inch white sidewalls. It met with enthusiastic public response when it appeared on the auto show circuit in 1960, and its innovative design elements, such as the front fender and rear quarter treatments, left a stamp on Chrysler products in the early 1960s, including the Imperial and Valiant lines.

The May 1960 issue of *Motor Trend* magazine called the XNR Plymouth's "Idea" Sports Machine and noted,

These two photographs taken in Italy before delivery show the XNR complete with its chrome side pipes, but without the final wheels or the chrome 'XNR' logo in the hood scoop.

"The XNR is the first step in the development of a sports machine that will eventually be offered as a production model." Unfortunately, that was not to be, and the XNR was sold several years later to a new owner in Geneva, Switzerland, who soon thereafter sold it to the Shah of Persia (Iran). It appeared in *Life* magazine in a story on the Middle East in the mid-1960s and then apparently ended up in Beirut, where it miraculously survived the war, stored in a secret basement garage. It is apparently now fully restored by its current owners.

Assimetrica

On October 28, 1961, at the 43rd Turin Motor Show in Turin, Italy, Ghia displayed the Assimetrica. Designed by Exner and based on a Chrysler Falcon, it was a more roadworthy version of the XNR with a rather incongruous, conventional upright windshield that bisected the offset power bulge in the hood. It had conventional 2+2 seating, the same racing-style instrument cluster, and a toned-down fin. Under the hood, which now sported four chrome fins decorating the mouth of the scoop, was another Slant Six. However, it was in the front and rear treatments where the car differed most from the XNR. The single chrome headlight grille surround with eyebrows and headlights translated almost verbatim to the 1962 Dodge Dart and Polara, as well as a couple of Dodge hardtop "third generation" turbine coupes. It was also copied by Sergio Sartorelli in the St. Regis Valiant and the OSI Fiat 1500S coupe.

According to Bruno Alfieri's history of Ghia, the Assimetrica was sold to thriller writer and creator of Maigret, Georges Simenon. The car is now at the Chrysler Museum in Auburn Hills, Michigan.

1960 *Chrysler 250 Valiant*

Despite being the progenitor and champion of fins, Virgil Exner's preferred style, as we saw in his early idea cars, was cleaner, subtler. And so it was, when fins went about as far as they could, he returned to simpler styling saying, "We of course turned to the idea cars which had been the product of our earlier creative efforts."

This shift was exemplified in the 1960 Valiant—Chrysler's entry into the small-car market. According to

Top right: Virgil Exner's May 1959 sketch for the front of the 250 Valiant. It's interesting to note how many details remained unchanged, including the tapering crease line in the side.

Several grille treatments were tried, including this intricate mesh as well as the egg crate grille shown above in a photograph taken by Ghia in Italy. The Ghia car also had shorter turn signal protrusions and no rectangular side markers. It was also fitted with aluminum-rimmed wire wheels that were replaced with the chrome wires and wide white walls.

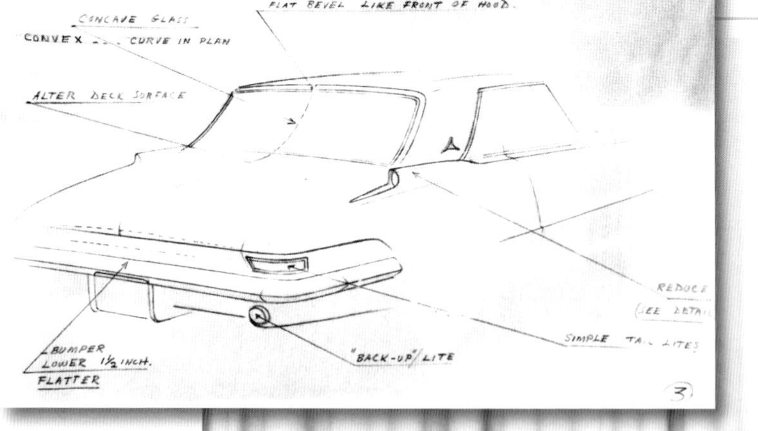

This sketch called for a "flat bevel—like front of hood" above the backlight as well as a reduction in the size of the abbreviated fins.

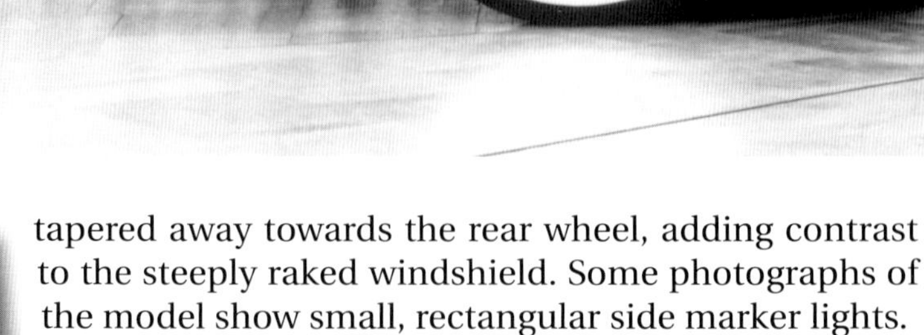

Bill Brownlie, "Exner wanted an elegant look as opposed to cheap—thus the six-window roof and Ferrari mouth." Had Exner's thwarted plans for the 1962 lineup gone ahead, a whole new look—Exner's fourth—would have joined the automotive design lexicon. Unfortunately, they were not to be. Hurriedly downsized, the production 1962s were quirky and consequently sold poorly.

To correspond with the introduction of the new '60 Valiant, Chrysler had Ghia build a concept based on a Valiant chassis. Called the Chrysler 250 Valiant, the two-door, four-passenger coupe took its name from the successful Chrysler 300 line.

In an Exner sketch shown in this chapter, dated May 10, 1959, the 250 featured some unusual styling cues such as protruding turn signals set above the single round headlights. The turn signals had gunsight "cross hair" trim ahead of the lens. These protrusions flowed back into the body, in a joining crease line that tapered away towards the rear wheel, adding contrast to the steeply raked windshield. Some photographs of the model show small, rectangular side marker lights.

Between the lights Exner had drawn a deeply recessed V-shaped grille with horizontal bars and vertical ribs, but different grille treatments appear in different photographs of the finished vehicle. There was no sign of Exner's signature heavy chrome grille surround.

The hood featured a recessed central valley with chrome 250 insignia at the front and tapered, chrome-trimmed louvers at the rear. There was, however, no sign of Exner's favored speedboat cowl. The greenhouse was elegant, with doors cut high into

the roof. However, on either side of the revolutionary split rear window—years ahead of the '63 Corvette—were oddly abbreviated fins. The fins contained taillights in heavily chromed "fish mouth" bezels resembling those on the 1960 Chrysler. The decklid tapered away gently with nary a sign of the simulated spare. Even the bumper was quite conventional, as was the front.

Interestingly, Exner's accompanying rear sketch indicates a concave glass in the backlight. This technique was tried on the stillborn Plymouth Super Sport preproduction model intended for 1962. Exner's drawing also calls for the size of the fin to be reduced (which obviously it wasn't) and for a simple taillight, and backup lights imitating the front turn signals.

Each wheel opening was accented with a small flare and chrome trim that helped highlight the 15-inch center-locked chrome wire wheels capped with white-wall tires. In a photograph taken by Ghia in Turin, Italy, the car is fitted with aluminum rimmed wires, probably from Borrani, and black-wall tires.

In many respects the Chrysler 250 Valiant was a landmark design. But automotive design was changing rapidly at the time, and it unfortunately didn't get the exposure it merited.

1961 *Dodge FliteWing*

The beginning of the 1960s saw a dramatic change in automobile styling. The flashy fins of the 1950s were rapidly displaced by body shapes with a new sharp, squared-edge look producing yet another crop of radical, stylish, and fascinating cars. Chrysler's new look featured large greenhouses with bold grille elements and crisp bodylines. The Dodge FliteWing was intended to set the theme for all the corporation's 1962 passenger cars. While some of the FliteWing's design cues appeared on the Valiant, Dart, and Fury in 1962, the theme was largely discarded when president William C. Newberg forced Virgil Exner to develop downsized Plymouth and Dodge

Though FliteWing would be one of Virgil Exner's last collaborations with Ghia, design cues first seen on the car did show up in subsequent production models.

Left and below left: Designated K300 in surviving Ghia materials, the FliteWing almost set a new trend in Chrysler styling. It was powered by a 383-ci "Ram Induction" V-8 producing 330 hp at 4,800 rpm.

Below right: What was perhaps Virgil Exner's boldest grille up to this time incorporated elements of the Falcon in its shape, but it had a heavy chrome surround.

As the door handle was activated, electric motors in the trunk operated the windows through flexible shafts. The windows were cut well into the roof. A tape pressure switch on top of the door prevented accidental closing on hands.

This wraparound and padded dash featured an early attempt at digital instrumentation. There were 13 elliptical windows showing speeds up to 130 mph in 10-mph increments. Brushed aluminum trim continued into the doors and was repeated in the seat frames and on the console.

intermediates. Newberg had apparently overheard that GM was downsizing the 1962 Chevrolets.

Exner used the opportunity to initiate design characteristics that today form the major factors in design worldwide: 1) shortened rear overhang, 2) lengthened front, 3) intensified wedge shape in side view, and 4) windows as flush to the sheetmetal as possible. Unfortunately, costly curved side glass wasn't used in the intermediate car lines, and engineering couldn't achieve the flushness shown in the FliteWing and Turboflite (detailed in the following chapter). Nevertheless, he did establish those principles in the 1962 designs.

Before Newberg's crash program railroaded Exner's production plans, the FliteWing took shape at Ghia. Built on a 118-inch wheelbase production chassis, FliteWing was powered by a 383-ci OHV "Ram Induction" V-8. According to specifications issued at the time, the engine, fitted with dual 4-barrel carburetors, produced 330 hp at 4,800 rpm and 460 ft-lbs of torque. Power delivery was handled by an early TorqueFlite automatic transmission.

With its shield-shaped, heavily chromed grille and integral front bumpers, FliteWing was decidedly different from what had preceded it. Nevertheless, it incorporated Exner trademarks such as the large 300 insignia stamped into the decklid, as well as wildly innovative ideas like the windows that extended up into the roof, which featured pronounced ridges running front to back.

Studio engineer Dana Waterman remembered, "The power-operated windows were designed to ease ingress and egress by opening high into the roof. The inboard roof rail provided greater head clearance; the styled ridges on the roof provided space for the four-bar power-window linkage, operated through flexible shafts by motors located in the trunk. The windows went up when triggered by the door handles or the tape switch along the beltline; closing the door closed the windows. The design goals were a glass surface flush with the sheetmetal (one of Exner's prime aims) and improved visibility through the large vent-window and elimination of any B-pillar frames."

The interior evidenced further safety engineering with heavy dash padding. The padding was sculptured with styled accent ridges and brushed metal inserts, which flowed smoothly across the entire instrument panel and into the doors. The instrument cluster was designed for readability and style with a centrally mounted speedo, which utilized a series of 13 elliptical "windows" to display the speed in 10-mph increments. Studio engineer Dick Burke recalled it as an early "digital-style" speedometer.

The normal dash controls were conveniently placed with the transmission push buttons in the leading edge of the fascia to the left-hand side of the cast-aluminum, two-spoke steering wheel. The other controls for turn signals, lights, antenna, and wipers were placed in a control panel mounted in an aluminum panel on the driver's door just ahead of the handle.

Four contemporary-styled bucket seats were framed in brushed aluminum and trimmed in top grain leather. There was also a long center console, which did not connect with the dash. It contained the air conditioning controls, ashtray, radio, and an armrest.

In November 1961, Chrysler President Lynn Townsend brought in Elwood Engel from Ford as corporate vice president of design. Exner took early retirement and opened an industrial design firm with his son. In his oral history, Virgil Exner Jr. said they opened/rented space from Luckenbach & Associates, an architectural firm on Woodward Avenue in Birmingham, Michigan, in 1962.

Although Exner remained a consultant with Chrysler through 1964, the 1962 Dodge and Plymouth and the 1963 Chrysler were his last production designs for the corporation.

Richard Burke *Studio Engineer 1957–1965*

"I was hired in through the Chrysler Institute of Engineering—there were 105 in our class. I spent the first three months in various engineering groups, one of which was in styling. I enjoyed it there and asked my supervisor, Hans Hierta, if I could stay. I worked as an engineer in various studios, including the Valiant studio under studio manager Richard G. Macadam, who eventually succeeded Elwood Engel as vice president of design in 1974.

"Ex had the front office, and there was a room behind that where he did his modeling. A door from that room led into another modeling area where I worked drawing up the basic surfaces from which we developed the engineering. I would also do suspension studies and other things for Ex. Ex was fun to work for, but he smoked too much.

"One of my tasks was to work on the mechanisms and electronics of the FliteWing as a mechanical engineer. I had little electrical engineering background, and consequently we had a lot of problems. The circuitry and mechanism for activating the side windows as well as the door latch triggering mechanism was very complex. For example, to prevent the window from crushing your hand we used a sensitive tape switch. I worked with Dana Waterman on that. Eventually we had it refined and approved by Electrical Engineering. Even so, I remember that Engel took the car home one night and neglected to check that the windows were fully closed. They weren't, and the battery ran down as the

closing mechanism ran all night. Elwood wasn't very happy when the car wouldn't start. We never did have a chance to work out all the bugs."

Window operating and door latch mechanisms were very complicated. A tape switch was used to prevent hands being trapped by the closing window.

A large box in the trunk contained door/window relay circuitry and battery charging components on either side.

1961 *Chrysler Turboflite*

Chrysler had been experimenting with automotive turbine power sources since the early 1950s, using production-bodied sedans for testing. For the 1959 season, however, Chrysler displayed this technology in a turbine-powered concept car, and the Marina Green metallic Turboflite became a landmark. Not only was its design radically different from production automobiles, it was also Virgil Exner's final show car.

The highly sculptured four-seat body was designed by Jack Kenitz in Maury Baldwin's studio and built in Turin at Ghia. It featured an aircraft-style, green-tinted canopy. The heat-deflecting front windshield glass wrapped around past where the "A" pillars would normally end. There were two separate tilt-out side windows, and the rear window was a low, wide opening framed by the built-in roll bar, which also acted as the structural pivot for the roof.

The overall design shows strong Virgil Exner influences with its cut-away front fenders, floating hood, and unique headlight arrangement, which in a modified form appeared in the '61 through '63 Imperial lineup.

Four red flashing lights warned occupants of the roof being lowered, but the action could be aborted by simply pressing the tape switch, a safety device mounted at the belt line at the top of the doors and quarter panel. This automatically stopped the lowering and returned the roof to the fully open position.

The leather-trimmed interior was designed around four extremely light, shell-backed, satin-finished aluminum bucket seats cantilevered off a centrally mounted structure. An air conditioning system changed the air every minute to keep the occupants comfortable, while a soft blue-green glow from the electro-luminescent door trim panel inserts bathed the interior.

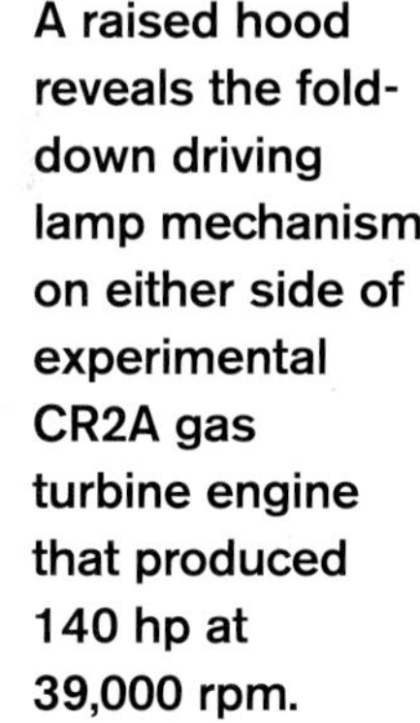

A raised hood reveals the fold-down driving lamp mechanism on either side of experimental CR2A gas turbine engine that produced 140 hp at 39,000 rpm.

Four aluminum-framed bucket seats upholstered in blue fabric and green leather flanked the transmission tunnel.

Instruments were clustered behind the steering wheel; below the tachometer was a pyrometer that measured temperature at the air intakes.

The dash featured a 50,000-rpm tachometer mounted to the right of the centrally mounted speedometer. Below the tachometer was an exhaust pyrometer, while the steering wheel featured a rim-mounted horn activation ring.

The rear of the Turboflite was dominated by a rear wing supported on a pair of vertical fins, each housing a stop light with day and night intensity settings. Between the fins was a "deceleration air-flap," which pivoted up into the airstream when the brakes were applied, creating additional air drag and reducing the load on the conventional braking system. Mounted in the rear edge of the air-flap was an amber deceleration light that illuminated when the throttle was lifted. Also, a large rear-light assembly illuminated a wide area behind the car when reverse was selected. The normal running lights featured a broad taillight panel across the rear of the car incorporating the turn signals.

The rear was equally innovative, with two-stage stop lights mounted in the tops of the fins and a pivoting deceleration wing complete with deceleration amber light and full-width taillights with back-up lights.

Here one can clearly see the dramatic lighting of the interior, where both the instruments and the door panel are illuminated.

The cast aluminum wheels were innovative, using an integral brake drum with wheel spokes designed as a centrifugal brake cooling impeller. By showtime, the tires not only had whitewalls but also a white ring running down the center of the tread.

Power was to be provided by an experimental CR2A gas turbine producing 140 hp at 39,000 rpm. It was lighter, smaller, and easier to build than a conventional V-8, required 80 percent fewer parts, and did not need a liquid cooling system. It also got better gas mileage than a contemporary Dodge. It differed from earlier turbines in having a new fuel-nozzle mechanism that varied the angle of the jet stream to the turbine blades, providing real engine braking, improved performance, and reduced lag. Earlier turbines took seven seconds to spool up from idle to full output, but the CR2A took only 1.5 to 2 seconds. The transmission was a modified TorqueFlite. According to Dana Waterman, senior studio engineer on the project, "There is no question that the Turboflite was a pushmobile with a dummy engine. It was never intended to run."

Lack of motive power notwithstanding, the Turboflite was the hit of the auto show circuit that year. Not only was it a cutting edge design that produced several production design cues, but it also offered a glimpse of the future that could possibly include automotive turbine power.

Dana Waterman   *Advanced Studio Engineer 1955–1965*

"An apprenticeship at General Motors in the Body Development Department of GM Styling taught me draftsmanship while working on the Motorama cars; I joined Chrysler in 1955. Where I had been designing convertible tops and seat mechanisms for Wildcats and Corvettes, I now began working on advance projects under Chief Stylist Cliff Voss in the Chrysler/Imperial studio. These years were a wonderful time of turmoil and innovation in automotive design; I was floored when Cliff Voss first showed me the 1957 Chrysler production clay models. They made the advance show cars I had been working on at GM look like yesterday's mashed potatoes.

"Reorganizations were frequent at Chrysler in those days, and in the next one I went to Maury Baldwin's new Advanced Studio at Outer Drive. We did many advanced body seating and configuration proposals there, culminating in the Turboflite, a startling showpiece for Chrysler's turbine engine. I did all of the engineering drawings for the body structure, including the drop-down headlights, the deceleration brake, the seating, and the powered canopy. The canopy was an aircraft-inspired design, with great visibility and excellent entrance room for such a low roof. Electric screw jacks lifted the windshield and the entire canopy, controlled by the door latches and a complex circuit of relays and switches. There were four safety tape switches located at belt height on the doors and quarters to sense the presence of a hand or arm and send the canopy back up before injury could occur. We had to design the complete circuitry; Electrical Engineering didn't want to touch it. After we had the breadboard working, they checked it over for us and made a few improvements before shipping it off to Ghia with the rest of our layouts.

"Working with electrical relays showed me how trouble-prone they are in complex circuits, and I began investigating the new reliable solid-state switches that were then coming into use. As a result, when the corporation began preparing for the computer age in the 1960s by building a three-dimensional digitizer for recording clay model surfaces, I was selected as liaison for Design Office to the Computer Center. This initiated a new career for me in supervising computer-aided design, beginning with the installation of the digitizer and continuing with the development and training of the CAD engineers and draftsmen needed to create the digital surface database for Design Office.

"My ultimate goal in this was always to provide the corporation with greatly expanded capabilities for the development of valid new design proposals, a goal which has now been achieved long after my departure. We were sometimes too far ahead of our time."

1962 *Dodge Dart Lancer GT*

According to DaimlerChrysler designer Jeffrey I. Godshall, writing in the December 1996 issue of *Collectible Automobile*, "The 1962 line was to be styling vice president Virgil Exner's fourth opportunity to redesign all of Chrysler's standard-size cars in the same year."

Godshall went on to say, "The basic design theme of the '62 Plymouth (and the rest of the all-new-but-never-to-be 1962 corporate line) came from a special concept car produced in strict secrecy, at Exner's request."

The reason for the new direction was sliding sales. While the 1957s had garnered Chrysler almost 20 percent of the market, sales subsequently began to erode; the corporation lost money for the first time since the Depression, and Dodge's new compact Lancer (a close relative of the Plymouth Valiant) was not well received—sales for all seven Lancer models didn't reach 75,000 in 1961. The Dart outsold it two-to-one, and even the Valiant managed a respectable 144,000 units. To give the model a little boost before it was killed and to introduce the GT, a mildly customized hardtop coupe was built for the auto show circuit.

New for 1962 was a more pointed grille. However, unlike its siblings, the GT had vertical bars. Under the hood was the new die-cast, all-aluminum 225-ci Slant Six, producing 145 hp. There were also slight changes in trim, and the show car enjoyed unique interior fabrics as well as a folding sunroof—from then on a recurring theme in Chrysler concepts. The car was also painted in a non-production metallic finish.

Sadly, it did little to boost sales. The GT accounted for a little over 13,000 units out of a total Lancer production of less than 65,000. It was the end of the line.

Fitted with a sliding fabric sunroof and optional model, it was hoped the Lancer GT show car would boost sales. Unfortunately, sales fell, and the Lancer brand was killed off.

1962 *Dodge Turbo Dart-Plymouth Turbo Fury*

Pictured with the Dodge Turbo Dart (left) and the Plymouth Turbo Fury is George J. Huebner Jr., executive research engineer for the Chrysler Corporation. Huebner had directed the gas turbine development program since its inception in 1945.

Hot on the heels of 1961's wildly styled Turboflite, the corporation's previous gas turbine experimental/show car, the company installed its latest generation engines into a number of Dodge Darts and Plymouth Furys and put them to the test.

One Dodge made an endurance run from New York to Los Angeles, and returned 17 mpg. This was actually quite good, because John Lawlor, writing in *Petersen's Complete Book of Plymouth, Dodge, Chrysler* said, "When I added up my gas receipts—or, rather, my kerosene and diesel oil receipts—and figured them against corrected odometer readings, I found that the car [one of the 1963 test fleet] had delivered 11.5 mpg."

The cause of the increased mileage was the new CR2A engine, which apparently returned better mileage than the piston engine of the conventional Dodge control car traveling alongside.

Of the various experimental cars built for 1962, two—a Dodge Dart and a Plymouth Turbo Fury—were specially prepared for public showing and debuted in January 1962. Both were two-door hardtop coupes.

The Dodge, displaying the license plate GT 3333, was painted light blue and had a large map of the United States, complete with the coast-to-coast route, on its rear quarters. The Plymouth, displaying the license plate GT 4444, was white.

The Dodge differed from its production sibling in that its grille was deeply recessed and fitted with twin turbine nozzles—matched by the wheel covers. Polara-style trim was also added to the hood sides, and it ran the length of the vehicle.

The Plymouth was likewise modified with the addition of a different grille—one that had "Plymouth" set asymmetrically to the passenger side. In the center of the hood was a heavy chrome ornament that read "Turbo Fury." There was a similar trim spear that ran the full length of the vehicle.

Both vehicles had upgraded interiors with bucket seats front and rear, upholstered in contrasting fabrics. Though good-looking cars, their fame would soon be overshadowed by the Elwood Engel-designed, Ghia-built 1963 turbine car.

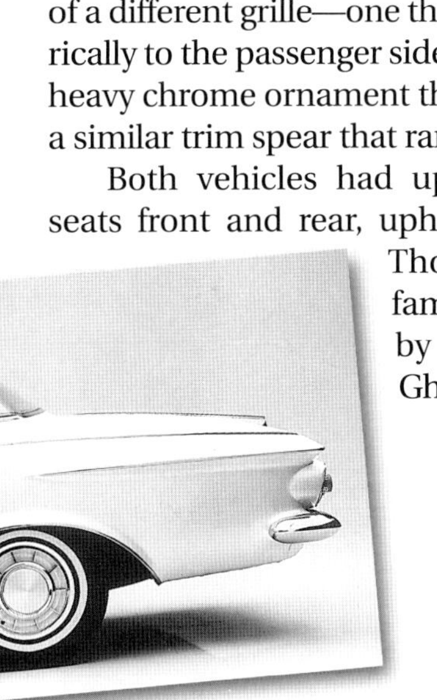

1963 *Chrysler Turbine*

"The Car of The Future" was the descriptor used in reference to the Chrysler Turbine when it was unveiled at Essex House in New York City on May 14, 1963. The event signaled the public launch of Chrysler's plan to build 50 such cars and have the public test them under everyday conditions.

Customer reaction tours of CR2A-engined turbine cars had been held in 1962, and later that year the company announced it would build 75 cars for public evaluation. That number was eventually scaled back to 50—nonetheless an ambitious program.

The story behind the car's design is far more fascinating than its powerplant, which the testing public

The interior rendering was the work of Bill Dayton. The turbine theme ran the length of the interior with all the controls in easy reach of the driver in the console. The dash featured a composite of three instruments set directly in front of the steering wheel.

The original "Typhoon" Turbine concept was this two-seater coupe by Chuck Mashigan, with large scoops in the side. These disappeared in the four-seater while the vents behind were moved forward to the front fender and reduced to three.

ultimately deemed too thirsty and lacking in power. In 1960, after ousting William C. Newberg from the presidency, chairman of the board Tex Colbert hired Lynn A. Townsend as administrative vice president. Once his feet were under the desk, Townsend voiced his dislike for Virgil Exner's designs, and in particular his latest penchant for debuting new styling ideas on low-priced models like the Valiant instead of top-end models. Despite profits of $11 million in 1961 (and $65 million in 1962), Townsend began to talk about a different direction and in November hired Elwood Engel from Ford.

Engel, who had been passed over at Ford, now became vice president of styling. Exner would continue for a time as a consultant. Meanwhile, according to Dana Waterman, Maury Baldwin was initially assigned to design the turbine car. Waterman, who was with Baldwin at the time as studio engineer, said in a recent interview, "Maury tried hard to point out that the relatively low-powered, slow-accelerating turbine engine would perform poorly in a conventional production car. It wouldn't fit the high-tech, jet age image of a turbine engine. Baldwin was proposing a small mid-engine two-seater along the lines of the Fiat

X1/9. Evidently, he didn't consider, or hadn't been told about, the coming 50-car test-drive program, for which the two-seater would have been ill suited. It was about this time that Chuck Mashigan came over from Ford and was assigned to the Advance studio.

"Engel wanted something like a Thunderbird and kept telling him, 'Come on Maury, get hot!' and Maury kept refining his little rear-engine job. Finally, Bob Bingman, who was at a level between Maury and Elwood, told him that he couldn't keep on being diametrically opposed to the boss's direction. There was a heated discussion and the upshot was that Maury was removed and offered a grade-8 job with Chuck Mitchell in Interiors. He, of course, turned it down and left the company to set up a successful design shop on his own.

"Sometime after his arrival at Chrysler, Chuck Mashigan was called up to Elwood's office. When he got there, Elwood opened a book to a certain page and said to Chuck, 'You know that one all right, don't you?' Chuck said, 'I sure do; that's a fiberglass T-Bird model I did while I was in the Ford studio.' Engel told him, 'Well, we're going to put a turbine engine in that car, Chuck, and you're going to be in complete charge of the body design.'"

Of course, Engel, as vice president, has always been credited with the design, which, because of its similarity to the Thunderbird, was often nicknamed the "Engelbird." Credit notwithstanding, Chuck's initial design was for a two-seater coupe complete with turbine references on the head and taillights, as well as the hubcaps.

The two-seater design was quickly parlayed into a four-seater, which retained the turbine motifs. Finished inside and out in Turbine Bronze, the 50-or-so four-seater two-door hardtops were built by Ghia in Turin, Italy, and shipped to Detroit, where the "fifth-generation" engines were installed. Incidentally, Luigi Segre had died unexpectedly that February. Assembly in Detroit was slow with about one car being built each week.

About 40 were loaned out for consumer evaluation, 203 people having been selected from 30,000 who

Elwood P. Engel poses with one of the 50 or so more conventionally styled four-seaters that resembled the theme of the '61 Thunderbird/Continental designs. Built of steel by Ghia, all but nine were crushed when the program was completed. Chrysler retains three cars; the other six reside in various museums around the world. Three are operational.

applied to Chrysler to be part of the pilot program. The first was delivered to Mr. Richard Vlaha in Broadview, near Chicago, in October 1963. Chrysler took care of servicing plus insurance and running costs, but the consumer was expected to pay for fuel, maintain the appearance, and complete the evaluation paperwork.

In all, over one million miles were racked up during the program, which lasted until 1966. The styling was the number one compliment, but drivers also liked the ease of starting no matter the weather. They appreciated the mechanical attributes of the engine, but about one-third of the users complained about inadequate performance, especially slow acceleration from a standstill.

Perhaps, when all was said and done, Baldwin had been right, and a small, lightweight two-seater was what was needed to sell turbine power to the public.

Chuck Mashigan *Design Leader, Advanced Studio*

"My wife suggested that I ought to design cars. I said I couldn't just start designing cars, I had no training or experience with automobiles, but she said, 'You've always liked to draw cars, and even model them in soap bars, and you do it well. You show them your work, and they'll hire you.'

"I made up some drawings and applied at GM, but I had no experience and they wouldn't hire me. I had no luck at Chrysler either, but I took my drawings to Ford (in a shopping bag) and was accepted for a 90-day probationary period. I reported to Alex Tremulis in an advance studio, where I did some sketches and even some modeling.

"After about 40 days, Alex called me into his office and said I had been requested by both the Ford and Lincoln-Mercury studios. That was 1954, and some months later I was told that Ford Division had requested that I go into the Thunderbird studio, and I was reassigned there as supervisor.

"One day, in 1961 or 1962, I got a call from Elwood Engel asking me to come over to Chrysler. Not long after I arrived he called me up to his fantastic office—rough stone, tropical plants, dramatic lighting, and bubbling waterfalls—a very different environment from the studio. He opened a book to a large photograph and said, 'You remember this, that's for sure. You developed it and designed it at Ford.' I had done it when I was in the Ford studio, and had been in charge through the design, the full-size clay, the fiberglass finished model, and everything. Elwood went on, 'Here's why I called you up here: I want you to design that vehicle to be a full-size running car, and we're going to put a turbine engine in it. You'll be in complete charge of getting that vehicle designed.' So this turned out to be the Chrysler Turbine car project; I did a two-seater first, with a long deck, and the second model was a four-seater with a longer passenger compartment.

"Some years later, Dick Teague, with whom I had worked at Chrysler, enticed me over to AMC, where I was in charge of the advance studio—I was there 18 years—and worked on the Marlin, the AMX, and the Pacer."

The rear view featured twin jet-like exhausts flanked by "boomerang" taillights and heavy chrome trim.

1963 *Plymouth Satellite*

While Elwood Engel's influence over design was beginning to be seen as early as 1963, there were some elements of the production cars that clearly harked back to Virgil Exner's era. For example, the front end of the Plymouth Sport Fury had vertical chrome bumperettes set at the leading edges of the fenders—a feature Exner had explored on many of his earlier designs. Nevertheless, his influence was waning, and Plymouth, like Dodge, displayed a more conservative, squared-up look. This look was evident in the new-for-'63 Sport Fury, which heralded the introduction of Plymouth's bored-out Max Wedge, resulting in the awe-inspiring 426 "Super Stock" producing 415 or 425 hp, depending on carburetion.

To showcase its new developments, the company rolled out a modified production show car, at the Chicago Auto Show, that unfortunately did not appear to garner much interest. Built by Creative Industries, it was barely covered in the contemporary automotive press, and one authoritative source gave it scant attention saying, "The Satellite convertible, a show car, was seen this year."

The majority of the modifications were performed on the interior of the car, where the standard bucket seats were replaced with over-stuffed seats covered in Pearlescent Shell White leather with Pearlescent Blue accents. Pleated and buttoned, they looked like they came from a luxury car, and this theme was carried

The interior of the Satellite convertible show car was where the effort was exerted. A full-length console that terminated in a tachometer split four luxurious leather-covered bucket seats.

A tonneau cover complete with fairings for the rear seat headrests helped turn the new-for-'63 Sport Fury into the Satellite show car.

Overstuffed bucket seats were another change made for the Satellite show car.

through to the door panels. The rear seats had headrests that were enclosed in fairings built into the fiberglass tonneau cover. Dividing the seats was a full-length console that curved up to meet the dash below the radio. At the end of the console, in easy sight of the driver, was a tachometer.

The other four round, black-faced gauges were located in a nacelle behind the steering wheel. This nacelle also contained push buttons for the transmission and other controls. The steering wheel was a two-spoke design, the top 60 percent of which was clear plastic—an unusual feature.

Externally, the Satellite was less dramatic and was almost production down to its hood decoration, quad-headlight grille with horizontal bars, full-length side trim, sill moldings, and bumpers. Where it did differ was in the lack of wipers and a top. Also, there was chrome trim capping the doors, tires with double white lines, and hubcaps with turbine-vane styling complementing the Iridescent Blue finish.

The new look had an obvious impact in the market-place, and while only some 15,319 Sport Furys were sold in 1963, the standard Fury model sold 69,503 and the division sold a healthy 488,448 vehicles. Chrysler was on the road to recovery.

1964 *Dodge Charger I*

Success in NASCAR, with Richard Petty, and Super Stock drag racing, with racers such as "Dandy" Dick Landy, had pushed sales of the Dodge Polara in 1964 to just over 45,000 units in both the base and 500 models. To celebrate this success, Dodge took a production Polara convertible and turned it into the first generation of three Dodge Charger concept cars.

Unlike most previous show cars, the Charger I was constructed in the manner of a traditional custom car, that is, by modifying an existing production car. This method of construction started a new trend that became popular later in the 1960s and into the 1970s. However, the other two Charger concept cars that appeared during the following five years were totally new and very radical designs, although in truth Charger II was actually based on a yet-to-be-seen production model.

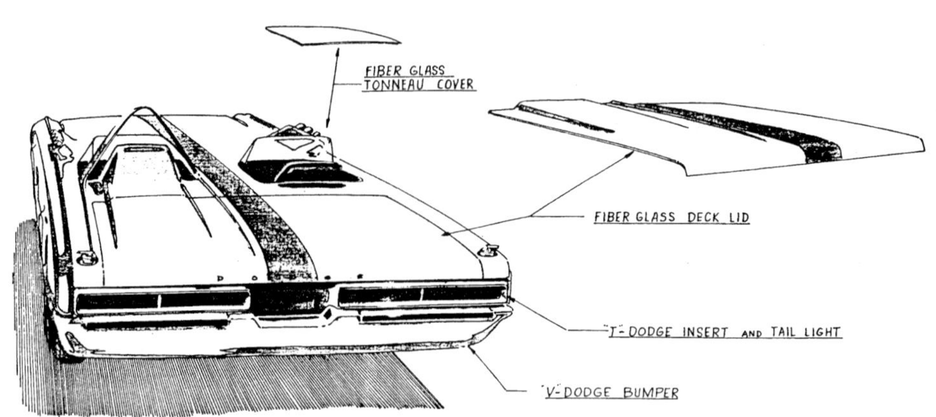

Cashing in on the company's racing success, the Charger I show car was built by modifying a production Polara. It was fitted with Dodge's 365-hp 426-ci Hemi, Halibrand-style racing wheels with faux knock-offs, and functional side exhaust outlets that added to the racing style.

The Polara's clean lines made the creation of the Charger I quite simple. The roof was removed and replaced with a molded roll bar that incorporated twin integrated headrest pods capped with vinyl-covered front pads, giving the car a sci-fi speedster look. The roll bar buttresses also tapered away along the top of the fenders. The rear seating area was eliminated, and the rear deck now extended all the way up to the back of the seats and beyond, for the cockpit was split into two completely separate seating positions.

Other major external changes included the low, "competition-height" windshield that wrapped around into angled side glass, which in turn tapered back toward the rear. Rectangular exhaust ports that could be uncapped to allow better breathing for the Hemi, if it was drag raced, were built into the rear quarters just ahead of the rear wheels. Also, the bumpers were replaced with bumperettes, the front and rear fascias were redesigned, and a small racing-style outside mirror was attached atop the driver's side fender. Incidentally, the interior mirror was replaced with a dash-top-mounted 8,000-rpm tachometer.

Finally, an open-scooped hood covered one of Dodge's new 426-ci Hemi V-8s rated at a massive 365 hp with its single 4-barrel carburetor. However, the Charger was engineered to also accept the Ramcharger 425-hp twin 4-barrel carbureted Hemi. Two racing stripes ran out of the scoop, down the hood, and continued under the front fascia.

Measuring 206.5 inches overall, with a wheelbase of 119 inches, the wheel packaging featured custom Halibrand-style magnesium wheels with fake knock-offs equipped with a set of special white-wall Goodyear Wingfoot high-performance tires. The design options allowed for installation of wider slicks for drag racing.

Even though the Charger I was but a customized production Polara, its significance as a concept car is remarkable—it offered a cost-effective way of taking show cars from the drawing board to the show floor.

Plymouth Satellite II

Chrysler's fortunes continued to rebound in 1964. However, there still seemed a scant budget for show cars for the Plymouth division—despite sales in 1964 of 600,000 units—and the Satellite II was therefore, again, a modified production Sport Fury.

No doubt overshadowed by the introduction of the Barracuda, the '64 Sport Furys sported a new, sleeker roofline. Possibly to highlight this, along with the company's landau-style vinyl roof treatments, the company cut the center section right out of the show car. This left what newspapers of the day described as a "landau canopy," which, according to the company, "Reduces wind turbulence for rear seat passengers."

The top was covered in black vinyl and was presumably (it was one piece) a two-person job to lift off. Also, it emulated the simulated landau tops offered on the '63 Chrysler New Yorker Landau and the '64 Chrysler 300 "Silver Special." The landau feature eventually offered on the Dodge Dart for 1965 proved a very popular extra, particularly on the GT models.

Other modifications from the production car included a slightly different grille treatment, "Plymouth" spelled out across the front of the hood, and no side trim. Instead, the wheel wells were connected with narrow chrome trim that ran along the top of the sill. The hubcaps had a turbine flavor, and the hood center trim retained its ornament. The quarter windows and the external door handles were also retained, giving the car a production look.

It was in the interior where the majority of the modifications were made. A full-length console separated four bucket-style seats. The rear seats had low-level fairings built into the parcel shelf. Each of the seats was covered in gold leather and nylon-faced fabric to match the gold exterior. The seats were also trimmed in hand-rubbed walnut accented with chrome trim. This theme

was carried through to other interior components, door panels, an so on, including the steering wheel.

According to John Lee, writing in Krause Publications' *Standard Catalog of Chrysler 1924–1990*, there was a Barracuda landau sister car to the Satellite II. When John saw the Barracuda, the car was being offered for sale at the Antique Automobile Club of America's Eastern Fall Meet at Hershey, Pennsylvania, and the owner had documentation proving that the car was indeed a factory show car and not an after-market conversion. The whereabouts of both cars are unknown at this time.

Gold on gold was the theme of the Sport Fury-based Satellite II. However, the removable roof section was covered in black vinyl. Inside, fairings were built around the rear bucket seats, which like the fronts, were trimmed in gold leather and nylon-faced material with chrome-edge hand-rubbed walnut accents.

1965 *Dodge Charger II*

Elwood Engel—hired in the fall of 1961 from Ford, where he had designed the '61 Lincoln Continental—knew what was coming from Ford and countered it with the '64 Plymouth Barracuda, and hot on its heels, the Dodge Charger.

The production Charger was based on a design by a senior designer in the Dodge Studio, Carl "Cam" Cameron, that was tagged "Monte Carlo" and was built atop the 117-inch wheelbase Coronet platform. Chrysler designer Jeffrey I. Godshall joined the company in the

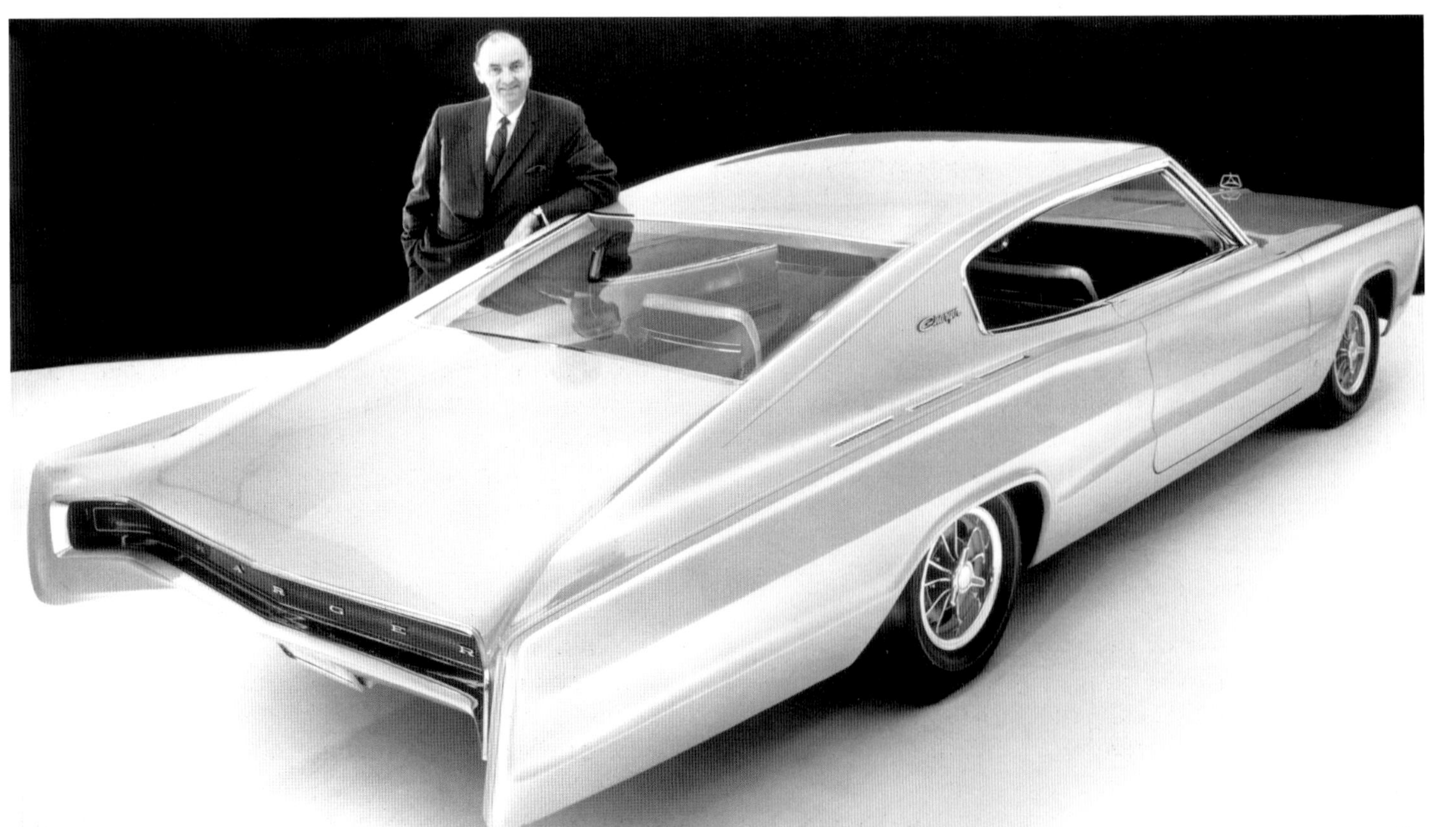

Elwood P. Engel, Virgil Exner's successor hired from Ford as Chrysler's new vice president of styling, leans against the gracefully tapering fastback of the Charger II. The design of the production car, which preceded this show car, was the work of Carl "Cam" Cameron, and it featured this flamboyant rear end with elongated rear quarters.

spring of 1963 as the project was in progress. Writing in *Collectible Automobile* in December 1998, Godshall said, "Culturally, the two fastbacks from Highland Park, Michigan were part of a revival that was gathering momentum in the mid-1960s. And, in a fortuitous concurrence, stock car racing was also back, a precursor of the muscle car era just over the horizon."

The Charger was to be part of that new vision as "The Leader of the Dodge Rebellion."

"Though their functional disadvantage remained," continued Godshall, "fastbacks once again meant speed and style. A team led by product planner Chuck Kelley, his boss Burt Boukamp, and Dodge Chief Designer Bill Brownlie was charged with making the proposed fastback variant as distinctive as possible, yet retail for under $3,500."

To whet the appetite of potential customers, the Charger II show car was developed to come out about a year before the production car. While it gave away the game of the fastback theme, some design elements of the production car, such as its rotating headlamps, were kept

secret. Instead, Charger II had a bumperless front end that featured a more forward-leaning profile, with corresponding reveals in the fenders. Single, rectangular lamps flanked a grille with four horizontal tubular bars. The whole assembly was surrounded by chrome trim.

The greenhouse was unchanged, but there were no wipers, no quarter windows, no door handles, and no external mirrors. There was also no sign of the production trim that would embellish the tops of the fenders, the wheel openings, and the sills. The pressed-in simulated louvers, a signature of the production rear quarters, were also absent.

The rear was equally different and here the design followed Cameron's original concept much more closely. The sweeping, fastback design flowed back into elongated rear quarters. Between them was a full-width taillamp assembly trimmed in chrome and carrying the word "Charger." The license plate was boxed into the bumperless lower fascia.

Overall, Charger II measured 215 inches, almost 11 inches longer than a production Charger. It was fitted with Halibrand-style mag wheels with imitation knock-off hubs similar to the Charger I. However, in place of the Charger I's thin white walls, Charger II rolled on redlined Goodyear tires. Under the hood was the ubiquitous 426-ci Hemi.

The Charger II would tour the auto show circuit before the production Dodge Charger appeared, and did so with great success. The new fastback styling was readily accepted by the public, paving the way for a significant new player in the Dodge Rebellion.

1965 *Plymouth XP-VIP*

"Win on Sunday, sell on Monday" was the sales-man's adage in the mid-1960s, when size and horsepower really mattered. Muscular engine options such as the Race Hemi, Super Commando 426, and the 415-hp Super Stock 426 "Wedge" pushed Chrysler to top honors with such notable wins as a 1-2-3 at the 1964

It could be said that the Plymouth XP-VIP featured the ultimate T-top. It created a wonderful canvas for the interior designers.

Floating bucket seats were upholstered in white leather as was the console, and the classic TV show *Sea Hunt* was on the screen.

Daytona 500 with Richard Petty leading at the wheel of his famous '64 Fury hardtop.

As important as racing was, there were venues other than racetracks. For example, the Mobil Economy Run, where Plymouth won honors in Class E when a Savoy returned an amazing 29.29 miles per gallon.

With the new AP Series being introduced, and the VIP planned for 1966 to combat Chevrolet's Caprice and Ford's LTD, Plymouth Division looked to up its stakes in the mid-luxury market. According to Colin Neale, director of interior design, "They commissioned the XP-VIP concept car from styling. The Exterior Studio made proposals for interesting front and rear end revisions of a production AP Satellite, and very kindly proposed an open-top concept that provided great exposure for the interior. This opportunity was grasped by the Advanced Interior Studio, and spearheaded by Dave Long they produced a highly sculptured, driver-oriented interior loaded with luxury features to support the VIP image." It is interesting to note that the cleanness of the interior was a milestone, and its influence would be seen many times over later years.

Known as the XP-VIP, its most innovative and obvious feature was the replacement of the conventional convertible top with a unique transparent roof supported by a central, longitudinal beam. This beam housed a track in which panels of photochromatic glass—to keep the interior cool in bright sunlight—slid up and down with the rear quarter windows to form a complete glass roof. The two main roof sections consisted of three panels, each of which could be retracted into the trunk.

The angular body differed greatly from contemporary production vehicles with its vertically mounted rectangular headlamps and lack of any real bumper or air intake. Small rectangular vents mounted low in the front pan were repeated in the rear. There was no discernable bumper in the rear either. Complementing the color-changing glass was a two-tone paint scheme featuring a unique, iridescent magenta paint on the upper half, which changed from magenta pink to brown, depending upon the way in which light struck it.

The interior of the VIP, designed with entertainment and the businessman in mind, was trimmed in white leather with highly sculptured shapes. It had a center console fitted with a dial radiotelephone, stereo, reel-to-reel tape recorder and, out of view of the driver, a TV for the passenger. The passenger seat could be rotated to face the rear compartment, which featured another TV along with a sound system and refrigerated refreshment cabinet. The VIP also employed a TV rear-view system. Interesting dash instruments featured a gauge predicting the flow rate of fuel at the driver's present speed and another predicting the estimated time of arrival based on the driver's travel inputs.

The XP-VIP was an interesting design that, although it didn't herald any major production ideas, did strike a chord with future Chrysler designers, who took minor touches of its cleanness to heart in the design of the '68 Plymouth Sport Fury's front end.

1966 *Chrysler 300X*

The importance of the Chrysler 300X was the fact that it is one of the few primarily interior-oriented show cars in the industry's history to date, and it is a car that accurately forecast in 1966 the dominance today of molded interior trim components. It was also unique in that the interior was done first.

According to Colin G. Neale, who had joined Chrysler from Ford as director of interior design, "Credit must go to a visionary vice president of sales at General Tire and Rubber, responsible for the Molded Products Division. This man, Dick Ault, had the idea that their research and development in making molded parts should be in lockstep with the wish lists of their OEM customers. After following protocol through Purchasing and Interior Body Engineering departments, he eventually wound up in my office. The chemistry was instant— the game was on."

Studio engineer Al LaCroix recalled problems with plastics. "At that time, expanded vinyl had a surface texture very similar to leather and was impervious to moisture. However, it had one weakness (this was more than 30 years ago): If it was sewn with the usual cotton thread, the tension of the thread on the surface layer would split the material at the seam."

Neale added, "We committed to making a design concept statement projecting our thoughts for the fully molded interior of tomorrow, and General Tire committed to make the interior components by processes that would explore new materials and manufacturing methods.

"We started from a clean sheet of paper, the first step being to think about and list ideas appropriate to tomorrow's passenger car needs. This was effected by having scores of 3x5 cards pinned to a 20-foot-long blackboard,

followed by a studio jury evaluation. This then led to a concept sketch.

"At this stage it seemed like a good idea to meet with our vendor partners, so we staged a major presentation of ideas under consideration. The exhibits included full-size package drawings articulated to show the various models, a quarter-scale model of the interior, and various illustrations of styling themes. This was all displayed in the Styling Showroom of the old engineering buildings on Oakland Avenue.

"We were on the frontier of interior design, with authentic support from a major supplier, and were able to bring some challenging ideas into reality. For example, with the help of Fred Hudspeth, a talented British engineer at Chrysler, we put together a twist-grip hydroelectric

Dick Ault (left) of General Tire and Colin Neale, director of interior design, discuss their plans for a revolutionary molded-vinyl interior for the 300X.

steering system that at the touch of a button retracted into the instrument panel for ease of entry/exit, or it would collapse during impact. Another new feature was the seat-mounted armrest, which retracted into the seat cushion. The seat belts also retracted into the seat structure. This provided total flexibility for door design, and also assured that the armrest was always in the correct ergonomic location for passenger comfort, wherever the seat might be positioned; we patented the idea.

"There were many other features, including a key-card ignition system; position adjustable, pressure-sensitive, oversized accelerator and brake pedals; a tape-recorded audio clock; a swiveling driver's seat for ease of ingress and egress; a reversible front passenger seat for interaction with rear seat passengers; an instrument cluster having the left side displaying vehicle information, and the right-hand side showing rear-view imaging with traffic-related information superimposed; and a rotary shift device on the console.

"As this exciting project grew into a full-size wooden buck, we realized that we had an extremely valuable property, but that it was incomplete. Consequently, I approached Phil Buckminster, then vice president of Chrysler sales, and suggested that a modest expenditure for enhancing a Chrysler 300 body shell would provide him with a high-content car for the show circuit. Phil gave his blessing, and his successor, Bob Anderson, eventually presented the 300X at a media event in Palm Springs."

Stan Johnson designed the exterior modifications in John Schwarz's Chrysler Exterior studio. The main change was the removal of the roof, the filling of all the window channels, and the addition of a wraparound windshield with a slight peak and a narrow chrome surround. In the front there was a unique grille and sectioned bumper that wrapped around the fender and ended in a delicate spear. The grille would be copied for the following year's production 300. In the rear, there were new quarter panels, a new decklid, and new taillights relocated in the chrome bumper. In place of rearview mirrors there was a Bell & Howell "Wide View Special Electric Eye" camera in the decklid, and both doors had magnetic passkeys.

Getting to Palm Springs was no easy matter, according to LaCroix. "The vehicle had a hundred stories starting the day I rode down the assembly line at Chrysler's Jefferson Assembly Plant. I literally sat on the hood of the vehicle with a series of charts describing which components were to be kept and which were to be deleted. Many of the assembly line workers were quite upset when I wouldn't allow 'their' component to be installed. And one man wouldn't create the additional welds we required to compensate for the elimination of some structure. The plant manager had to come to this man's station and get another worker to add the required welds. There were no production interior trim parts left in the vehicle, and no top or windows, so we had to create a special bag in which to ship the vehicle by normal rail shipping.

"Meanwhile, the entire interior had been clay-modeled, including the seats. General Tire fabricated all the vinyl trim components, and then they were shipped by rail to Modesto, California, where they were to be assembled by custom car builder Gene Winfield."

The seats were most unusual. According to Wally Wyss, writing in Petersen's *Complete Book of Plymouth, Dodge, Chrysler*, "Instead of the springs used in ordinary bucket seats, the 300X buckets had rubber-nylon diaphragm suspension. The driver used a rubber air cell to adjust the seat height." Of course, the front seats also had the built-in armrests as well as head restraints, which eventually found their way into production. The rotating feature of the front passenger seats and the blue neon interior lighting didn't see production.

A collapsible steering column was eventually adopted for production, though not in the form explored on the 300X. However, the Chrysler-engineered twist-grip steering did not catch on, nor did the Bendix zero-travel brake and accelerator. Something that did find a place in many modern automobiles was the console-mounted TV; it was soon to be followed by the rear-view monitor.

"To prepare final assembly, I went out to Winfield's with the electronics engineer and the research engineer," said LaCroix. "We pre-assembled the entire vehicle and painted Prussian blue on all the metal parts and scribed in the grid

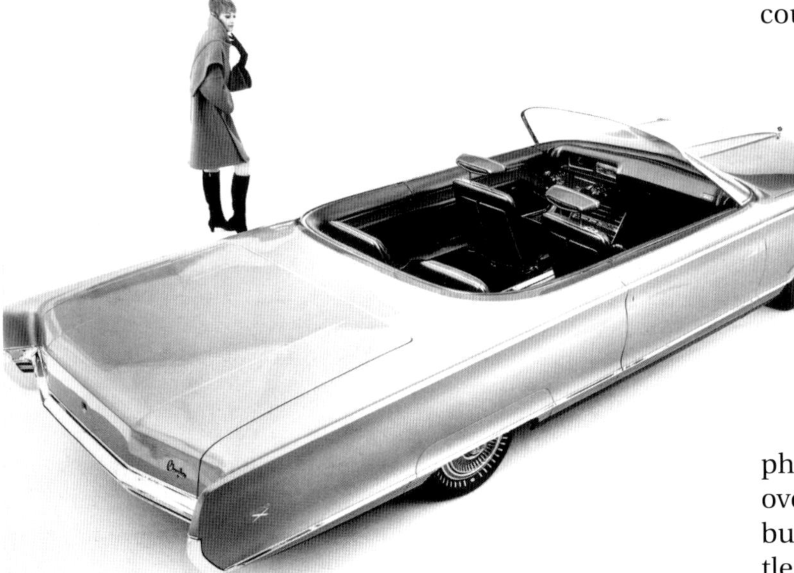

locations for everything. All wiring harnesses, seats, trim panels, etc., were marked with their corresponding identifications. Everything was ready for the Chrysler Financial and General Tire executives to visit and see the product they had paid for. No problem, right? Wrong! After we left, a well-intentioned mechanic sprayed black paint on the sheetmetal parts, hiding all the wiring harness markings and trim installation locators.

"Back in Highland Park [Michigan] I reported to Colin Neale that all was in readiness for their final approval to finish the vehicle for the press release in three weeks. Now the executives arrived in Modesto to discover the vehicle in complete disarray; there was no way for Winfield to determine where to attach anything. Colin called me to his office and sent me packing back to Modesto to sort it out.

"The day after the 300X was completed, to be sure that the vehicle was safe to be driven by Chrysler executives and the press, my mechanic and I elected to test drive the car on an abandoned country road. Suddenly, a farmer pulled out in front of us. I slammed on the zero-travel brake and my sunglasses flew off and disintegrated against the windshield. The brakes worked fine.

"Driving back to Winfield's we also noticed that the shift control felt very loose. And, as we loaded this quarter-million dollar car into the truck, it stuck in park: We could go neither forward nor backward. I found that the control shaft between the transmission and the "dial shifter" had cracked in half. It turned out that the machined shaft we had specified had been replaced by two cut-off socket wrench sockets silver-soldered back to back. The solder had cracked and finally broken. With the car on the ramp there was no way to get under it to make the repair. We had to jack it up and disengage the park sprag brake from under the center console.

"Eventually, we arrived in Palm Springs and the photography was done. But our problems were far from over. One of the neon lights in the rear compartment had burned out, and the only way to replace it was to dismantle the entire interior, remove the seats and the quarter

The 300X was laden with techno features from the hydroelectric twist-grip steering to the blue neon lighting, which ran around the passenger compartment.

panels, and take out the rear console. Then we had to get a neon sign maker to reproduce the tube, matching the specific blue, and reassemble the whole thing.

"Finally, we arrived at the golf course location of the press event only to find that the steering had given up and the car could only be driven to the right. As I was pondering what to do, Colin arrived and asked to drive the car to the front of the clubhouse. When I explained the problem he gave me some words of encouragement: 'Get the bloody thing fixed.'

"After we had figured out how to disguise the fact that it would only turn right, it ran out of gas. Eventually, we manipulated the car onto a circular path in front of the clubhouse. I drove the press around and around to the right, explaining to them that I wanted to restrict our movements to the cart path so that all the press people and photographers would have a chance to see the car in motion."

So began the career of the Chrysler 300X. After three years on the auto show circuit, Chrysler finally decided its usefulness was over, and it was scrapped.

A major feature of the 300X was its highly sculptured molded door and quarter trim panels, dramatized by the concealed neon lighting. Colin Neale remembered, "Naturally, we wanted to bring these ideas to the marketplace; our initial effort was on the 1970 Barracuda and Challenger doors. All we were able to achieve at the time were the sculptured door and quarter panels, but funding would only allow inexpensive, hard polypropylene for the material. It would be many years before material and process technology, together with the necessary allocation of funds, brought us to the luxurious soft-sculptured doors that we enjoy today… as was forecast by the 300X."

Those concepts, along with pressure-sensitive braking and dial shifting, were not features that ever made it to production, but the 300X's pioneering molded-vinyl upholstery did appear in the '70 Barracuda and Challenger.

1967 *Dodge Daroo I & II*

Not all of Chrysler's concept cars of the 1960s were built in the traditional Detroit manner. For example, the Daroo I was built by George Barris at Barris Kustom City in North Hollywood, California, under the supervision of Dodge's chief stylist Bill Brownlie. The name was apparently a derivation of the early Anglo-Saxon word "dar-u," for a dart or spear and, according to Brownlie. "We wanted to convey a feeling of a real dart in motion even while the car was still standing still. The intent was also to give a tough performance image compatible to the styling concept."

Using a '67 Dodge Dart GT convertible as a starting point, George built the "Daroo I" in less than four months, during the summer of 1967. The re-engineering

and customizing was extensive even though Barris did not alter the stock 111-inch wheelbase or the drivetrain. He did, however, remove the convertible mechanism, extend the nose 17 inches, and cut 10 inches off the tail. The overall length became 202.4 inches. With the roof gone, George lowered the windshield and beltline so that the Daroo sat just 42 inches high.

The grille was heavily V'd and featured headlights hidden behind brushed satin-finished horizontal bars. Below, the front pan was rolled in true hot rod fashion and fitted with tunneled driving lights. Above, the hood was adorned with eight spectacular-looking cold air induction rams; unfortunately, they were not functional.

Daroo I was powered by a 383 with a 4-barrel and a 4-speed manual transmission.

King of the Kustomizers, George Barris, flanked by two Chrysler staffers, sets up the fake ram tubes. These forward-facing tubes were later changed for vertical stacks when the Daroo I was repainted candy orange.

The windshield and side glass continued the V theme. It was created in a medium charcoal tint, non-glare process to contrast with the Daroo's first color scheme of Pearl Honey Yellow paintwork with black bumblebee stripes. Accenting the paint were black side pipes and chrome five-spoke wheels shod with Firestone tires.

The tapering profile was continued to the rear with full-length windsplits that culminated above another full-width bar grille disguising wall-to-wall taillights and sequential turn signals. Round backup lights matched the front driving lamps and were tunneled into the rolled rear pan.

The two-seat interior was a combination of stock and custom parts, and included a four-on-the-floor shift lever, a deep-dish steering wheel, and a driver-oriented central instrument panel that looked very added-on. The deep pleated custom seats were covered with coarse-grained ebony vinyl and featured air inlets, adjustable leg lifts, and built-in headrests.

The Daroo I: was first shown at the fourth annual Santa Clara County Motor Car Dealers auto show, Wonderful World of Wheels. It became such a hit on the show circuit (where it was described as "Daroo I A Show Car Happening From Dodge") that it was repainted candy orange for the 1968 show season, and candy green with straight rather than angled stacks for the following year. The Daroo I is now part of the Steven Juliano Chrysler Muscle Con-cept Car Collection in Pelham Manor, New York.

Daroo I's final guise as part of Steven Juliano's collection.

Dodge Daroo II

The interior featured bright orange upholstered half-buckets, deep-dish wood-rim steering wheel, and angled tachometer.

A Daytona-style front end featured deeply recessed headlamps behind square grating, Virgil Exner-style floating chrome bumper, and brushed metal stripes. Note the restored car does not have the Dodge lettering in the grille.

Also surviving, and part of the Blackhawk Collection at the time of this writing, is the sister car, the Daroo II. It, too, was a two-door, two-seater with a cut-down windshield with no header or wipers. However, it had a targa-style top but no roof insert. Rather than the V theme of the Daroo I, Daroo II somewhat predicted the styling of the Dodge Charger Daytona of 1969 with its wedge-shaped front end and kick-up in the rear. It even displayed the Scat Pack racing stripes around the tail.

The front end featured three deeply tunneled apertures with headlamps hidden behind square, three-dimensional mesh. The grille contained letters spelling out "Dodge" and was separated from the headlamps by recessed, brushed metal grooves that ran from the thin chrome bumper, over the hood, and all the way back to the cowl.

The grille treatment was repeated in the rear, where it ran the full width. Also repeated was the

The rear view of the Daroo II clearly shows full-width taillight assembly, rectangular exhaust tips, twin racing-style gas filler caps in heavily sculptured decklid, and headrests floating below the roll bar.

narrow, Virgil Exner-style bumper. Twin racing-style fuel fillers adorned the sculptured decklid.

The interior likewise embraced the racing theme with rather short bucket seats upholstered in bright orange fabric. Matching headrests stuck out like arms cantilevered from an extension of the aluminum-trimmed center console. The console also housed a tachometer angled at the driver and mounted in a machined aluminum cup. Unlike the Daroo I, this car was an automatic and was powered by a 340-ci, 275-hp V-8.

Originally painted candy orange, not the red of the restored car, it rode on magnesium wheels instead of the chromed Cragar S/S five-spoke wheels shown. Also, the tires were Goodyear Blue Streak racing tires and not the Polyglas F-70-14s shown.

1967 *Dodge Deora*

The trend towards personal-use pickups was barely in the public's consciousness when renowned Detroit customizers Larry and Mike Alexander were commissioned to build the Dodge Deora.

At the time, Chrysler engineers, designers, and product planners felt that there would be a tremendous upsurge in the sale of vehicles based on a pickup format. They anticipated these vehicles of the not-too-distant future would combine the creature comforts of a luxurious town sedan with the sporty individuality of a European GT car packaged in the amazing utility of a pickup truck. With tonneau cover in place, Deora would serve as a personal car everywhere. With tonneau cover removed, there would be ample room for a matching "slide on" type camper unit for family recreational travel. Without the camper unit in place, Deora would be equally practical as a cargo carrier for the businessman, the homeowner, and the sportsman. History has proven them right, and at the time the company said, "Deora—far more than a stylist's dream—is the first bold step into the virtually unexplored field of the true sports-pickup."

Designed by Harry Bentley Bradley, who was at the time employed by GM but was moonlighting for the Alexanders, Deora was based on a Dodge A-100 pickup. It was chopped and sectioned from the stock height of 78 to just 57 inches tall and featured a unique split front door, the top half of which had actually seen service as the tailgate of a '60 Ford wagon.

The interior under construction displays the linkage that was used to operate the steering.

The finished interior.

Mike and Larry Alexander with the Deora. Mike went on to work for American Sunroof, while Larry went to Ford.

With a wheelbase of 90 inches, Deora measured 189 inches overall. It was 79 inches wide and stood 57 inches tall. It rode on custom-built deep-dish reversed chrome wheels fitted with 10.50x13 Firestone "Little Indy" racing tires.

Because of Deora's unique front-entry, the manifold vacuum, fuel, alternator, water temperature, and oil pressure gauges were mounted in a wood-grained panel located to the driver's left, just above the built-in armrest. All were fully functioning Stewart Warner custom instruments, as were the tachometer and speedometer housed in individual, self-illuminated nacelles mounted on Deora's custom wood-grained slimline center console.

The ignition switch, lamp switch, turn indicator switch, and power windshield control were located on the vertical steering mechanism post, facing the driver. Also located on the post was a release knob that allowed the steering wheel to swing out of the way for easier ingress and egress.

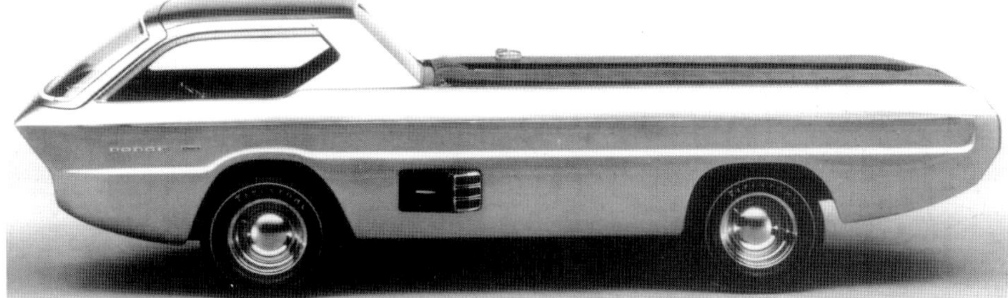

The stock 170-ci Slant Six was moved back 15 inches. The transmission was a 3-speed manual with Hurst shifter and linkage engineered by Hurst. Also located under the hard tonneau cover was the radiator—complete with electric fan—mounted behind the rear axle, and the gas tank mounted behind the cab.

The placement of the steering wheel offered the A Brothers, as Larry and Mike Alexander were known, a real challenge. While it was fairly easy to design a swing-

The Deora got is name after model car company AMT ran a promotion in *Car Model* magazine for readers to name the truck. Designer Harry Bentley Bradley had proposed XTAB for "eXperimental Truck, (Mike and Larry) Alexander Brothers," but David Hagedorn's Deora won the prize—a model of the truck.

away steering wheel, making it work posed a greater problem. The solution was to mount the wheel on a swing-arm built from sheet steel. A roller chain with a special constant-tension cam device connected the steering wheel to a vertical shaft that actuated a power steering unit tucked next to the left-front wheel well. The steering wheel itself was a regular American production wheel, cut down to form an aircraft- or dragster-style butterfly wheel.

The center console also contained the power windshield mechanism, comprising a 12-volt DC motor and control arms that pushed open the windshield, hinged either side at the top. In the down position, the control arms were designed to form a smooth, flowing continuation of the console. Double bull's-eye courtesy lights, on both sides of the console, illuminated the shag carpet.

While there were two locking lugs (one at either side), a single release button popped the center-hinged, swiveling door open at the touch of a finger. However, as a safety measure, the door could only be operated when the windshield was in the raised position. The door locked automatically when swung to the closed position.

Once inside, the driver and passenger could settle back into Naugahyde and carpet-covered fiberglass bucket seats separated by a floating armrest and featuring an ashtray with custom foldaway cover. Deora's engine compartment was positioned directly behind the armrest—the stock 170-ci Slant Six having been moved rearward 15 inches.

Externally, Deora was equally radical atop its deep chrome-reverse rims and Firestone "Little Indy" tires. The lines, however, were sleek, broken only by the exhaust outlets exiting through the bedsides behind the front wheels. They were, in fact, yet another Ford part—Mustang taillight bezels fitted with baffles.

One of the most interesting features of Deora was the taillight assembly, which consisted of a series of three sequential warning lamps on either side concealed by a rosewood accent panel that ran the width of the bed. The lamps, taken from a Thunderbird, were also hidden above a stainless steel panel that had been photomicroetched with thousands of tiny, conical, perfectly circular holes. This etching technique gave the stainless steel a solid appearance, yet allowed light to pass through unhampered, and the light actually reflected off the rear bumper surface. It was the finishing touch for a vehicle described by Wallace Wyss as, "Easily the best custom ever built—if you consider a 'factory show car' a custom."

1967 *Plymouth Barracuda SX*

Wallace Wyss, writing in Petersen's *Complete Book of Plymouth, Dodge, Chrysler* published in 1973, described the Barracuda SX as, "One of the slickest cars ever to come out of Chrysler's Design Studios."

Unfortunately, the SX, unlike its Barracuda siblings, was all show and no go. For while there was suspension and steering, there was no drivetrain under the sleek fiberglass shell. Nevertheless, when it appeared on the show circuit early in 1967, it did predict a number of design cues that would make it to production in the ensuing years.

The Barracuda first arrived in 1964 as part of the established Plymouth Valiant V-200 compact. Its signature sporty fastback roofline set it apart from the other Valiant models that included a hardtop, convertible, station wagon, four-door sedan, and two-door sedan.

But by 1967, the designers were reaching for high-er ground with ideas for a larger, sportier model. This up-scaling was first seen in the Barracuda Formula SX. Overall, it was about 20 percent bigger than the production Barracuda.

According to SX designer John Herlitz, who had just signed on with Dick Macadam in the Plymouth studio, "The first program I got to work on was the '67 Barracuda program. There were three different cuts that we were taking at that program: We had a complete re-skin of the Valiant; we had a fastback Valiant, the successor to the '64; and the proposal I

In this shot of the clay modeling process, John Herlitz is working on the driver's side front fender. Al Germonprez is alongside him, and Jack Avoledo is at work on the back. According to Herlitz, "Al and Jack were the key modelers on the SX program."

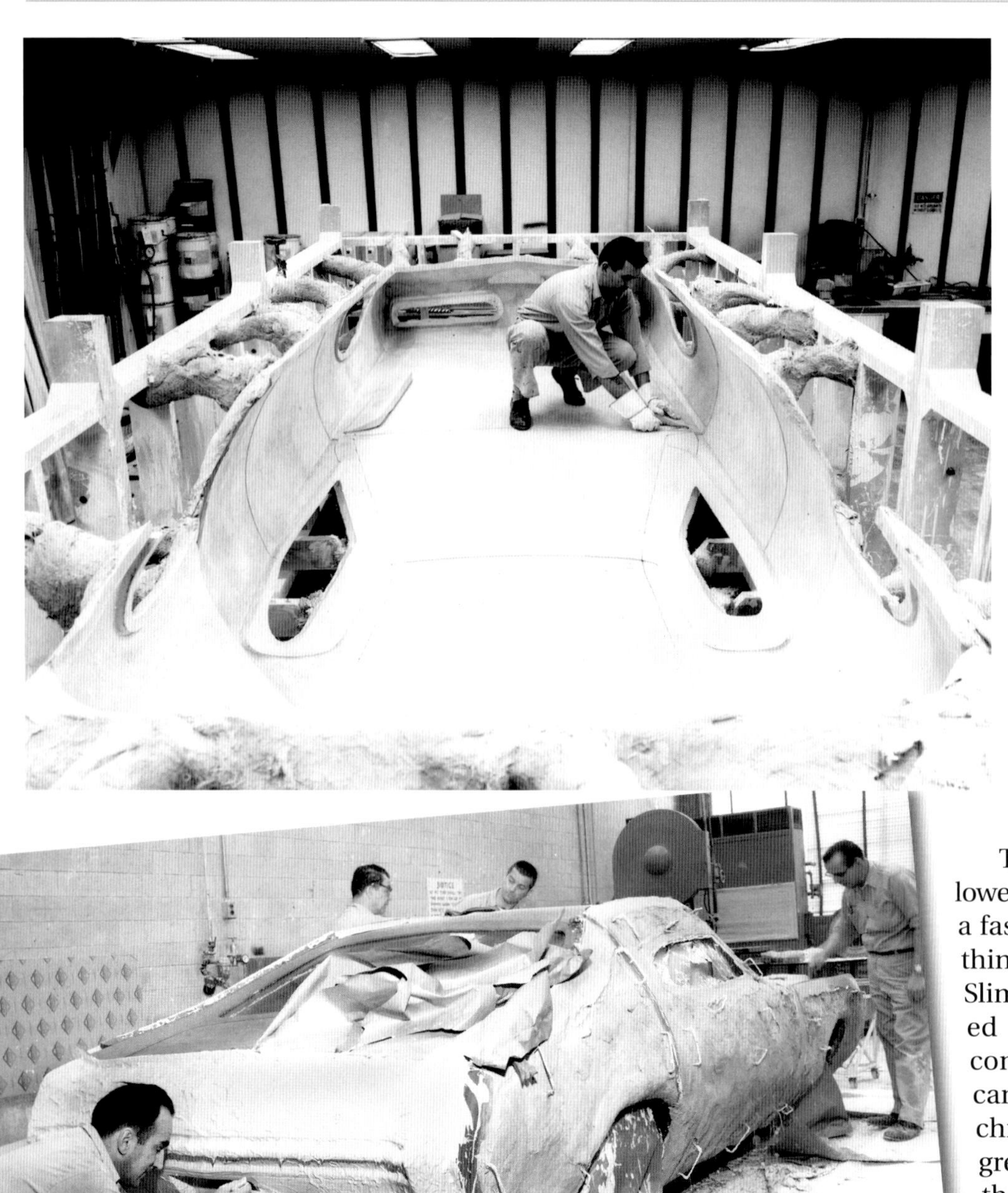

Left: This is the mold for the one-piece body.

ended up with Dave Cummins and Milt Antonick interpreting my design over the Valiant underbody, while I was off for six months of Air Force basic training.

"We made a fiberglass model of the original which we targeted for the Chicago Auto Show, but McCormick Place burned down on the eve of the show, so it debuted at the New York Auto Show."

The standard way to build concept cars was to mold the body in one piece. The window and door openings were then cut out after the body was finished. The windows were all formed of Plexiglas. It was a big job, and while model fabrication technology was gleaned from this project, little could be applied to production vehicles.

The SX had a clean profile, was slightly lower than a stock Barracuda, and featured a fastback/notchback design unlike anything Plymouth had previously offered. Slim A-pillars and flush door glass created a large, open greenhouse, raising comparisons with Virgil Exner's beloved cantilever look of the mid-1950s. While chrome trim would be added to the greenhouse, it hardly detracted from the lightness of the design.

The SX also featured a heavy chromed grille, again in the style of some of Exner's early idea cars that would, albeit in a modified form, go into production on several models, including the '70 Gran Fury coupes, sedans, and Suburban wagons. It was also used to more dramatic effect on the '71 Road Runner, which, of course, was

initiated was a totally new design. The company went so far as to investigate the purchase of a foreign manufacturer to build that design in January, but financially, it just wasn't in the cards. So it

also designed by John Herlitz. The bumper contained rectangular headlights as well as a pair of large round turn signals set in the middle of the opening. Photographs of the clay indicate another direction and profile for the grille aperture that didn't make the final cut.

The bumper treatment in the rear once again reflected Exner's influence. The taillights were built into the inside surfaces of both upper sheetmetal and lower bumpers. A heavy chrome section connected the two extremes and sandwiched a full-width black nerf strip.

Later photographs of the SX show "Plymouth" badges on both the leading edge of the hood and the lower por-tion of the decklid. The Barracuda logo of the "progress review" clay was also replaced with a simple SX logo shown on the finished car. There were also racing stripes that ran from the peak in the grille, through the hood and roof to the lower edge of the decklid. The American Racing-style five-spokes shown in some photographs were used for the final concept SX when it went on the show circuit. The car was always shown with red-stripe tires.

The finished vehicle. Notice the air vents visible here in the tops of the fenders, and the red stripe tires.

1968 *Dodge Charger III*

For the 1968 season, Dodge wanted a concept car to help fire up its "Dodge Rebellion" advertising campaign, so it set about reinventing the company's future with a program that led to the creation of numerous clay models, all of which centered around the canopy cockpit styling idea. When Dodge introduced the Charger III, it was heralded as, "A bold, new imaginative experimental car designed to significantly diminish the distance between the will of man and the response of the machine. Its every feature is aimed at providing instant response to the desires and commands of its two occupants—whether for comfort, convenience, enormous acceleration, tremendous speed, and long-distance mile-eating cruising."

As such, the Charger III marked a distinct change in company conceptualization of its future. Unlike the production-based concept cars, which had emerged from the studios in the early 1960s, the Charger III's sleek and chic lines turned the company's vision toward the next decade, using an exotic vision that had made the first Ghia-built cars so intriguing. Virtually every major design aspect of the Charger III was new and daring.

Designed by Jim Eberjer of the Dodge Exterior studio and built by Vince Gardner of Detroit on a 100-inch wheelbase chassis, Charger III featured a jet fighter-style canopy that tilted up and backwards at the touch of a button. As the canopy rose, the steering column, with its attached instrument cluster, lifted up and out of the way to the right, and the seats rose forward and up eight

The canopy lifted up and back as the seats raised forward and up eight inches. The steering wheel also rotated out of the way to allow ingress and egress. There were no rearview mirrors. Instead, a periscope mirror popped up out of the roof.

Contemporary magazines compared the Charger III to the General Motors Mako Shark, but it displayed numerous features that placed it in another technological category. Charger III measured 184 inches overall, was 73 inches wide, and stood just 42 inches tall. Large ducts in the hood were functional, as were those in the side that fed cooling air to the rear brakes.

inches. Once seated, the driver pressed a second button that reversed the procedure, closing the roof and resetting the steering wheel.

Because the side glass went up with the roof and because there was no rear window, there were no rear-view mirrors. Instead, another button released a pop-up periscope rear-view mirror mounted in the roof. The interior was also devoid of any instrumentation. Instead, in a recessed panel by the driver's left hand, there were elec-

tronic push buttons for lights, radio, heater, etc. What little instrumentation remained was located in a cushioned cluster below the steering wheel. The seats were high-backed buckets with integral head restraints. To keep passengers cool, fresh air was collected at the base of the windshield, circulated through the cockpit, and exhausted through the rear vent.

It was never mentioned what, if any, engine powered Charger III, but the February 1968 issue of *Motor Trend* claimed, "Any of the Dodge family of V-8s—even the 426-ci Hemi—can be fitted." Nothing was ever said about the transmission, either, but the shift lever indicated an automatic transmission with five forward gears and overdrive.

Whatever the engine was, it could be checked without lifting the hood—a service side panel built into the left-hand fender folded down, allowing easy access to check fuses and coolant, oil, and battery levels.

One feature that would be explored on subsequent Chrysler concepts was that of auxiliary air brakes. Three were built into the rear body and extended as the conventional disc brakes, the rear cooled by the side scoops, were applied. Pressure also activated a strobing rear stoplight. Also, under the upper flap were twin racing-style quick-fill fuel fillers. The wheels were of an interesting disc design, with deep-set centers and 8.00/8.20-15 Goodyear tires.

The Charger III toured the car show circuit with great success, and it is easy to understand how many of its features translated into several Chrysler production cars, including the '70 Dodge Charger and 'Cuda. However, its most innovative ideas never saw production, and it would be the mid-1990s before Chrysler built a production two-seat coupe with the Viper GTS.

Here, the pop-up periscope rearview mirror can be seen along with the three air brake flaps. Under the uppermost flap were twin fuel fillers.

1968-70 Dodge Topless/Super Charger

Often shown alongside the Daroo I was the Dodge Super Charger that, like so many of Chrysler's show cars of the time, enjoyed a varied history. What began as a '68 Dodge Charger R/T had, according to the October 1968 issue of *Car Life*, originally been modified for the personal use of Elwood Engel, Chrysler's vice president of styling, though Bruce Hatch is credited with the design.

To begin with, Engel had had the roof removed and the ensuing hole filled all the way to the back of the front seats, around which fairings, tapering far back along the decklid, were fabricated. The windshield was cut down 10-1/2 inches to match, and the glass was left frameless across the top. The glass channels in the doors were filled, and the door handles and decklid lift were removed. Long side pipes were added, as were racing-style outside mirrors mounted high on top of the fenders. In the rear, twin racing-style filler caps (only one was functional) were let into the tops of the fenders, and they were tied together with wraparound blue graphics. The front and rear bumper and bumperettes were painted body color. The hood, held down by racing-style quick-release pins, featured two non-glare graphic panels in the indents, with the driver's side displaying the numerals "440," a reference to the 375-hp 440 V-8 under the hood.

Rare photographs of the Dodge Topless Charger as it was originally converted by the Mike and Larry Alexander as personal transport for Chrysler's vice president of styling, Elwood P. Engel.

The roof was removed and the rear seats were paneled over. The front seats were given long, tapering headrests. A 375-hp 440 powered it.

According to the November 1968 issue of *Motor Trend*, other features of Engel's Charger included a perforated stainless steel steering wheel and five-spoke, 15-inch American Racing wheels (stock size was 14-inch) shod with Goodyear tires, and a stainless exhaust. The spare was tucked in the trunk behind the seats.

Close inspection of the photographs shows that medallions were affixed to the doors in the ends of the fake scoops—on the passenger side they were the Canadian and British flags. The builders of the Dodge Deora, Larry and Mike Alexander, carried out the modifications.

The Charger was such a hit that it was restyled by George Busti's Creative Customs for the 1970 season. Inspired by the racing success of the Daytona, the Charger was fitted with the Daytona's tapered nose cone, complete with flip-up headlights. Below was a built-in lip spoiler containing directional indicators.

The hood, still held down with hood pins, was given a black-painted center and featured vacuum-operated louvers to increase engine cooling. On either side were rear-facing air ducts to facilitate the expulsion of hot air from the brakes. The finned aluminum side pipes remained, but the emblems and graphics were deleted. Under the hood was the stock 375-hp 440-ci Magnum V-8.

In the rear, the filler caps remained, but the fenders were built up to form a full-width spoiler complete with a driver-controlled, electrically operated center section. It was wrapped in a simple black stripe.

What was now called the Super Charger was painted Fire Orange and rode on polished-aluminum, deep-dish five-spoke wheels. Inside, the seats were changed for higher-backed buckets, which no longer fitted the fairings as neatly as the originals.

At the time of this writing, the Dodge Super Charger was part of the Steven Juliano Chrysler Muscle Concept Car Collection.

Second time around, now known as the Dodge Super Charger, the Topless Charger R/T was restyled by George Busti of Creative Customs. Molded onto the front was a nose cone from a Dodge Daytona, of which only 505 were built for NASCAR racing. Also taken from the '69 Charger were the hood, here painted black and complete with vacuum-operated louvers, and the reverse-facing ducts for the expulsion of hot air from the brakes. The five-spoke American Racing wheels were changed out for polished slot mags.

The gas filler caps in the tops of the fenders were retained, but adorning the rear was a new spoiler that could be electronically adjusted by the driver.

1969 *Dodge Custom Swinger 340*

Initially known as the "Custom Dart Swinger Idea Car For Today"—a rather unwieldy moniker that was soon shortened to "Custom Swinger 340 by Dodge," according to the front license plate—this modified Dodge Dart was unveiled at the 1969 New York Auto Show.

Based on the A-body, the Custom Swinger 340 had been conceived as a tough-looking streetcar with race-oriented overtones. The concept sketch depicted a modified grille, functional-looking hood scoop, chopped top, racing mirrors, shaved door handles, scoops in the lower rear quarters, a racing-style filler cap in the rear fender, and a lip spoiler on the decklid.

Unfortunately, it is unknown whose shop modified the body. Nevertheless, they comprised a new grille insert made of fiberglass and fitted with rectangular Cibie headlights, and what were found to be Ford Mustang fog lamps during restoration.

The hood, held in place by chrome hood pins, was fitted with a dragster-style bug catcher described in the contemporary press releases as a "tri-clops scoop." It was, in fact, fabricated from sheetmetal, painted matte black, and fitted with three over-the-counter aftermarket exhaust tips—another fact discovered during restoration. To continue the smooth lines, there were no cowl vents or wipers. Under the hood was a stock 275-hp 340 V-8 with a 4-speed.

No doubt, the major part of the Swinger's construction was the six-inch roof chop, described in the factory literature as a "cantilevered roof"—no doubt a nod to previous idea cars. Apparently, the windshield was cut to fit, but the rear glass was simply laid down and the rear pillars modified to suit. Rather than go to the trouble of modifying the side windows to align with the lower top, the glass was removed and the channels were filled. The stock door handles were also removed and new, vertical ones were fabricated in the quarters.

Though not quite in the style of the rendering, racing-style mirrors were fitted to the tops of the doors. However, the scoops destined for the lower rear quarter panels in the sketch were never installed. The external filler cap was fitted and the decklid was given a small lip spoiler. During restoration by Ken Brambleet of Jamestown, Indiana, it was discovered that the spoiler had been fabricated entirely of lead. The decklid weighed in at 200 pounds. In fact, it was so heavy the

stock hinges wouldn't support it, and opening it caused minor distortion of the quarter panels. Consequently, once the trunk compartment was restored, the decklid was closed and left that way.

To match the front, a new recessed rear panel was formed and fitted with one-off, hand-fabricated lenses embellished with 1965 Pontiac surrounds. The side marker lamps were pirated from a '68 Chevy Chevelle. The restoration of the Swinger 340 also unearthed the fact that the rear bumper was, in fact, a stock 1969 Valiant front bumper.

The only other modification to the exterior of the Swinger was the installation of polished 14-inch aluminum Ansen Sprint wheels fitted with Goodyear Wide Tread GT tires and a candy red paint job, with signature bumblebee stripe around the tail.

The Custom Swinger 340 was not a huge hit on the show circuit and received scant media attention.

Consequently, at the end of the 1969 show season, George Busti of Creative Customs was paid $1,000.00 to repaint the car Lime Fire Pearlescent. After being stored for many years, the car was sold and is now part of Steven Juliano's Chrysler Muscle Concept Car Collection.

1969 *Plymouth Duster I*

The year 1969 was the pinnacle in the history of the muscle car. All the Detroit manufacturers were fueling the fire with increasingly powerful muscle cars that in reality were little more than Super Stock drag cars in street guise. Chrysler, a major player, had enjoyed an amazing decade of racing success in both NASCAR and NHRA drag racing, and to capitalize on its success, it developed the Duster I specifically for the show circuit. This stunningly aggressive concept, introduced at the Chicago Auto Show in 1969, was presented as a racing machine for the street.

Built around a heavily modified Road Runner, complete with torsion-bar front end, Duster I had its rear

Duster I had 16 inches taken out of its wheelbase for a total length of 186.7 inches. Also, the wheel openings were enlarged to accommodate H.60 x 15 Goodyear tires. The hood/fender stripe carried graphic representation of specifications, and adjustable spoilers molded into the corners of the fenders were supposed to reduce front-end lift at high speeds.

wheels moved forward until its wheelbase was a mere 100 inches—16 inches less than a standard Road Runner. This was a drag strip trend designed to improve weight distribution. These new dimensions resulted in a two-seater cockpit flanked by a chopped, frameless windshield and side glass that tapered back to the wide seats, which were molded into the rear deck. The seat nacelles housed frenched taillights. Above the seats was a roll bar complete with twin adjustable spoilers, which the driver could use to increase downforce on the rear wheels. A second set of "air brakes," not unlike those on Charger III, were built into the rear quarter panels—supposedly to control high-speed yaw. Each flap had a cutout to clear the racing filler caps.

The front end featured rectangular headlights in a deep-set, mesh-filled grille. Below were twin air ducts flanked by a pair of airfoil-section adjustable spoilers molded to the body. These were said to minimize front-end lift.

The hood sported a pair of side-vented cold-air inlets that were accented by black racing stripes inscribed with the engine specifications. The rear was likewise sans bumper but enjoyed Kamm styling treatment, with a pair of rectangular exhaust outlets set in the center of the rear panel. There was no trunk.

As was written on the fender, Duster I was powered by the 426-ci Hemi, with a production TorqueFlite automatic transmission.

Finished in a brilliant orange, Duster I had H60 series tires on deep-dish 15-inch wheels with a large offset to give them a racy look.

Duster I was quite a hit when it appeared, being described in *Motor Trend* as "Perhaps the most exciting street rod type of show car ever created by Chrysler.

1969-71 *Dodge Yellow Jacket/Diamante*

Dodge continued its recent policy of using production cars as plateforms from which to build its image cars with two cars in one: The Dodge Yellow Jacket that, in turn, became the Diamante.

The car began life as a production '70 Hemi Challenger convertible, apparently the first Hemi convertible E-body ever produced. It was black with a black top and a black interior, and came fully loaded with a 426 Hemi, 4-speed transmission with pistol-grip shifter, leather seats, rallye dash, power windows, power top, power steering, power brakes, and 4:10 gears in a Dana rear end.

The all-new '70 Challenger had only recently been introduced, but as desirable as the car was, Dodge wanted a two-seater to go against the Corvette. Journalist Jim Mateja, writing in the April 23, 1969 *Chicago Tribune* said, "Reportedly, Chrysler was planning to introduce this car as a Corvette fighter until accounting types put

pen to paper and estimated a production version would cost $15,000. The project was abandoned." In 1970, a production Challenger cost less than $4,000.

According to the "Inside Detroit" column of the January 1970 issue of *Motor Trend,* Dodge engineers dreamed up the modifications and shipped the car out to Ron Mandrush of Synthetex, of Dearborn, Michigan. In Ford's backyard, Mandrush transformed the convertible into a two seater with a targa-style top with a removable one-piece insert. A power-operated "Breezeway" rear window was installed, as was an integral chrome roll bar. The car stood 48.9 inches tall—two inches lower than a stock Challenger.

Externally, the Yellow Jacket featured Honey Gold pearl yellow paint, a pair of tape stripes that ran the length of the tops of the fenders and disappeared into the side scoops, side exhausts, and, of course, the legendary Shaker Hood.

The center section of the rear spoiler was also power-operated and could be controlled from the Challenger SE-level cockpit, as could the rear window. The spoiler ran the full width of the rear deck and was molded into the rear fenders. The taillights were prototypes of the factory's 1972 design. The car rode on Goodyear Polyglas GT tires and five-spoke alloy wheels.

In its original Yellow Jacket guise, the car sported a Shaker Hood under which resided a 426 Hemi with dual quads and a 4-speed. Originally, the car was painted pearlescent Honey Gold with two stripes disappearing into a scoop on the rear fender.

Unfortunately, as was the fashion at the time, Dodge introduced the Yellow Jacket to the public with a bikini-clad model whose body could be "painted" at the auto shows. As you would expect, the body painting was far more interesting to the crowd than the car, which basically "got lost in the crowd." Consequently, Chrysler executives were apparently disappointed with the car's poor reception and decided to have it restyled, at a reported cost of $250,000.

The corporation had the body repainted pearl white and displayed the car, now called the Diamante, without the body-painting gimmick but with more than $1 million worth of diamonds.

In fact, the car had been extensively restyled. Again, Ron Mandrush did the work. To be-gin with, the Shaker Hood was removed and replaced with a narrow hood that contained two rectangular scoops at the leading edge and louvers in the rear. The fender tops were widened to meet the

The interior featured leather seats, steering wheel, and console.

narrow hood and were fitted with flip-up headlights. According to Dave Duricy Jr. in the *Standard Catalog of Chrysler*, the roof was of fiberglass, as were the hood and front fenders. At some time, the doors were also fiberglass, but they were eventually replaced with steel. The nose was made of steel and Duraplastic, and the rear bumper was color-coated rubber.

The production-style grille was completely reshaped. Ribs were installed around the molded-in fascia, and the integrated bumper/grille was split and filled with horizontal bars and one rectangular driving lamp in each opening. The tape stripes were removed, and air outlets were added high up in the front fenders. However, the side pipes were retained.

In the original press kit rendering, the Diamante, also called the "Little Gem Show Car," was shown with the Yellow Jacket's five-spoke aluminum wheels complete with the F-60x15 Goodyear tires, but by the time the completed car was shown, it had been fitted with multi-spoke cast-aluminum wheels.

Dodge put out a press release at the time that said, "The design was developed by Dodge engineers in wind tunnel studies and tested in competition on the high-banked ovals of the NASCAR circuit." However, it is unlikely the Diamante ever saw the high-banked ovals of NASCAR. In fact, after its first showing, along with the new 1971 models, the car was badly scratched and was repainted. The job was given to George Busti of Creative Customs who, instead of the pearl white repaint they were expecting, gave Dodge a shocking Candy Tangerine job.

According to the current owner, Steven Juliano, the car was displayed until 1972, when it was put into storage. Six years later, it was sold at auction and eventually passed to Steven Juliano where it became part of his Chrysler Muscle Concept Car Collection.

Part of Steven Juliano's Chrysler Muscle Concept Car Collection, the Diamante was restored to its third and final iteration complete with candy orange paint and Goodyear Polyglas GT tires.

1970 *Chrysler 70X*

Unlike its contemporary idea cars, the mighty Concept 70X was oriented more towards the family or businessman, rather than the weekend racer. While some of its styling cues (for example, the narrow, almost full-width grille and flip-up headlights) would find a home on the front of the 1972 Dodge Monaco, it was the three sliding doors that predicted the shape of doors to come on Chrysler's minivans of the future. In a paper presented to the Society of Automotive Engineers in Detroit on January 12, 1959, Jack Charipar, chief engineer and director of products at Plymouth Division at the time, and the man who supposedly coined the word "imagineering" that same year, had said, "The doors in our 1970 car can be larger, lighter, and easier to enter, as windows might be fixed in curved door panels opening into air-conditioned interiors."

In fact, Charipar was 10 years ahead of his time with the Concept 70X when it was introduced by Richard G. Macadam early in 1969 in the Chrysler-Plymouth studio. It featured large, easy-to-enter doors that extended into the roofline and had fixed glass. Concept 70X also heralded the "Fuselage Look" and set the theme for the corporation's 1970 models.

According to Tom Gale, who worked on the car as one of his first major projects at Chrysler, "The car was done in fiberglass, and the night before we were to display it,

Heralding the "Fuselage Look," the 70X was a three-door concept with two doors on the driver's side and one on the passenger side, all operating on parallelogram hinges. Unlike other pillar-less concepts, there was a structural B-pillar as well as an integral roll bar. The doors opened some 15 inches from the car.

This might have also necessitated the long front overhang necessary to accommodate collapsible assemblies and increase occupant protection.

Other safety attributes included the proximity warning device on the inside rearview mirror (there were no outside rearview mirrors). When a vehicle behind approached within 50 feet, an ultrasonic device detected its presence and a light on the mirror indicated which lane it occupied. The 70X also contained side-impact beams, a built-in roll bar with mesh head restraints, and a combination seat and armrest between the two front seats that could also serve as a rear-facing child's seat.

the guys picked it up with a lift and dropped it. Boy, did we have to scramble. It was devastating; we had been working night and day."

Interestingly, the Concept 70X, much like Chrysler's early minivans, had three doors: two on the driver's side and one on the passenger side. All three doors featured parallelogram hinges so that they could, according to the contemporary press releases, "open outward and swing parallel to the car. They open some 15 inches from the side of the car and are ideal for tight parking situations." The two-door side had a structural B-pillar, the exterior door handles were located in the middle of the doors, and the glass was frameless on all edges. On the passenger side, the large single door glass was framed all around.

With such drama in the doors, embellishment typical of the day might have seemed unnecessary, and there was little chrome, no visible wipers, and no front parking lamps. There were, however, side markers and high-level brake lights, which reflected growing safety concerns as the result of the 1966 Highway Safety Act.

Inside, the instruments of 70X were hidden behind a dark, thin panel that ran the width of the interior and were backlit when the ignition was turned on. All the controls were placed on a steering wheel console within easy reach of the driver, while buttons to activate the indicators were mounted on the end of the spokes, much like some of today's horn buttons. In fact, the Chrysler Concept 70X displayed numerous innovations that would become mainstream.

1970 *Chrysler Cordoba d'Oro*

The beginning of the 1970s saw a new vision of the future manifested in concepts that were far more exotic than had been turned out during the previous decade. For example, the Chrysler Cordoba d'Oro, a Dart-like coupe with most unusual proportions, employed a cantilever roof that referenced the ill-fated Norseman. Press announcements of the time described it as "A smooth, pillar-less monocoque designed as a luxury four-place hardtop with a long-hood, short-deck body which features smooth uncluttered bodywork rolling down to fully enclose the rear wheels."

Made of fiberglass, the Cordoba d'Oro was finished in a metallic gold with a suggestion of a metallic brown undertone that helped create a warm, darker shading as the light changed. There was virtually no trim, save Chrysler logos on the front quarters and the decklid. The front-wheel openings were large but well filled with 15-inch five-spoke Halibrand-style alloy wheels and Goodyear tires. The doors, which extended up into the roof, were long and offered easy ingress and egress to

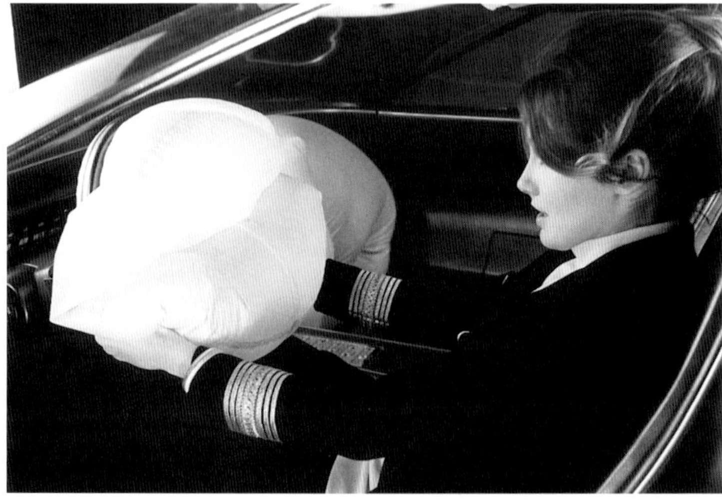

both front and rear seats. And, rather than conventional handles and locks, a combination lock using a five-number combination was used.

The front-end treatment, with its extreme "overbite," featured four rectangular openings containing

An early concept airbag—in the shape of lips—was never shown to the public. Colin Neale remembers that management thought that it was premature at that time to take a position on such a controversial subject. The experimental pedestal seats with integral lap and shoulder belts were trimmed in gold leather to match the exterior paint and mouton carpeting.

experimental headlights in the top and thermostatically controlled intakes for engine cooling below. Auxiliary to the headlamps were two high-intensity halogen high beams, and the grille area was framed with chrome.

In the rear, there was neon tube lighting that ran around the fender line and up over the rear window. There was also an air brake let into the rear of the roof that functioned in sync with the conventional brake system.

The four-bucket-seat interior was likewise unusual and innovative. Colin Neale, director of interior design, said, "Allied Chemical approached the industry with concept technology for an adjustable pedestal-base bucket seat with an integral lap- and shoulder-belt system. We created an elegant clay model, but unfortunately there was no further development until the Cordoba came along, when we built a complete interior around it. To this day, I don't think I have ever seen a complete interior designed with a more simple theme. We also installed an early concept airbag, slowing it down so that it could be safely deployed for demonstration purposes, but it was never shown to the public."

The Cordoba d'Oro also had a horizontal-style dash that featured an early mechanical/digital speedometer and a "Road Condition" indicator that rated the road surface condition: wet, dry, or icy. Other innovative ideas included a real-time TV monitor, referred to as the "Special Traffic Monitor," that replaced the conventional rear vision mirror, and a combination ignition/lock and Safety System that monitored all the Cordoba d'Oro's electrical and mechanical functions.

The whereabouts of the Cordoba are unknown at this time. It didn't have a great impact on production beyond some innovative technical features, which have since become commonplace.

Elwood Engel, Paul Malasky, Colin Neale, and Don Forman discuss their concept seat with integral safety belts.

1970-71 *The Rapid Transit Caravan*

ate in 1969, the concept of a touring display of modified Plymouth vehicles called "The Rapid Transit Display" gained corporate approval. It was hoped that the vehicles would inspire Plymouth owners to purchase custom accessories and high-performance parts for their own vehicles. The tour, which included replicas of Don "Snake" Prudhomme's Funny Car, was a huge success and visited major auto shows, dealerships, and special events across the country throughout 1970 and 1971.

For 1971, the original Road Runner was retired and replaced with the new 1971 body style. It, the Barracuda, and the Duster, which had carryover styling, were ordered restyled for the Rapid Transit Display. Once again, as in 1970, Harry Bradley was contracted to do the design work. Because of a tight schedule, the vehicles were given to several shops to be reworked in just six weeks.

The 'Cuda 440, as it was called, was the most extensively restyled of the four cars, the work being performed by Chuck Miller's Styline Custom of Detroit. Although the signature Shaker Hood was retained, the front end was extensively modified and extended by means of a nacelle set into the grille. Deep set were Cibie rally-type headlamps. The lower fascia was rolled

The 'Cuda 440 was extensively modified by Chuck Miller's Styline Custom. It was fitted with a 440 six-pack.

This is the Duster 340 in its final combination of candy greens and flat black. It was originally red.

under, and split spoilers were installed to the sides, with parking lamps below.

All handles and latches were removed and replaced with solenoid openers, while Trendsetter side pipes ran the length of the rockers. In the rear, the pan was modified to accommodate wheelie bars and a centrally mounted parachute. The rear window was reinforced with steel braces, and the car was lowered 2-1/2 inches.

The paint was a mixture of reds, pinks, oranges, yellows, and whites, all covered by Murano pearl. It was a good example of the panel-style popular at the time. The wheels were chromed Cragar five-spokes, 14 inches wide in the rear and fitted with Goodyear slicks.

The Duster 340 was sent to Byron Grenfell of Marquette, Michigan, where the front end was completely restyled. The bumper was made thinner using T-Bird and Camaro parts, the pan was rolled, and the stock headlights were replaced with Lucas units. The parking lights were relocated to the pan, and the hood was extended and emblazoned with the word "Duster."

Twin racing-style filler caps were set into the quarter panels, while the rear was restyled to match the front, complete with roof spoiler. Originally red, the paint was changed for 1971 to a combination of candy greens with flat black and hues of pearl. Butch Brinza, of Milwaukee, applied the paint.

Lowered three inches, the Duster 340 had chrome rocker moldings and polished Universal Regal wheels fitted with Goodyear Speedway Y-7 tires. Under the hood was a 340-ci engine with a 4-speed manual and a 3.90 rear axle.

This is the '70 Road Runner, complete with Road Runner graphics on the side, now owned and restored by Steven Juliano.

The '70 Road Runner was another thinly disguised stocker, which, unlike the other two cars, was raised three inches in the rear— "adding to the 'drag strip look,'" according to the contemporary press release.

The body modifications were performed by Roman's Chariot Shop, in Cleveland, where the shop fabricated a new plastic honeycomb grille and fitted nine-inch Cibie headlamps. Below, the bumper was graphically split and painted flat black to match the body side stripes, hood, and decklid. Under

The '71 Road Runner is complete with "chicken heads" that light up with the headlamps. The modifications included extending the nose and placing the headlights behind the grille, and a new fiberglass hood with cowl-induction scoops.

the power-bulged hood with a pop-up scoop was a dual-quad 426 Hemi backed up to a 727 TorqueFlite transmission and a 4.10-geared, drag racing axle.

Other body modifications included enlarged side scoops, a full-width spoiler mounted four inches above the functional decklid, a new full-width taillight assembly, and rear wheel wells flared four inches to accommodate the 14-inch-wide Ansen Sprint wheels and Goodyear tires.

The body sides were painted candy gold and adorned with scurrying, oversize Road Runners. The roof section was painted white pearl.

For the following year, Chuck Miller prepared a new '71 Road Runner, again to Harry Bradley's design. This time, the only items not altered were the doors, roof, interior, and horn, which still went "beep-beep."

The front end was extended more than six inches and incorporated a roll pan and a hand-formed mesh grille, behind which the headlamps were mounted. A new hood was made of fiberglass to incorporate twin ram-air induction scoops at the base of the cowl. Under the hood was a modified 383 V-8.

In the rear, the decklid was likewise made of fiberglass; its center recessed four inches with a spoiler formed between the fender tops. Below was another hand-formed pan that housed concealed taillights that showed green when in "drive," yellow when the car decelerated, and red when the brakes were applied.

The paint was a vibrant candy-over-pearl orange with a white-pearl break line that ran the entire length of the car. However, the most endearing feature of the 1971 was its three-dimensional, vacuum-formed Road Runner heads—described affectionately in the contemporary press release as "chicken heads." Mounted to the front and rear quarters, as well as the grille, they illuminated with the headlamps.

With the exception of the 'Cuda 440, these vehicles are part of the Steven Juliano Chrysler Muscle Concept Car Collection.